Take It From Me

A Man's Perspective

Sipho Mbele

Copyright © 2016 Sipho Mbele.

All rights reserved. No part of this book may be used or reproduced in any form or by any means, electronic or mechanical, including photocopying, recording or any information storage or retrieval system without written permission from the Publisher.

ISBN 13 : 978-0620716000

ISBN 10: 0620716002

Published by Classic Age Publishing.

Po Box 134, Braamfontein, South Africa, 2001.

Printed and bound by Hartwood Printers, Midrand, South Africa.

Edited by Vukulu Sizwe Maphindani for Classic Age Publishing
Cover Design by Classic Age Publishing
Website : www.classicagepublishing.co.za
Email : info@classicagepublishing.co.za

PREFACE

The two statements; *Am I loved*, and *Do I love?* Which usually causes us to contemplate what LOVE is gives a meaning to the question itself. Either we wonder, *am I loved*? Or we ask, *do I love?* It is therefore easier to first address WHAT IS LOVE as a result of the love we feel coming toward us. If we understand how to best apprehend when loved, we can also learn to identify our own love for others.

When loved, we feel it spontaneously in our guts. But how does it work? Is there an extrasensory perception in the heart that can read the feelings in another person's heart? It's really not that ethereal or supernatural. It's practical and down-to-earth. Our hearts take cues from our senses. Everything we see, hear, taste, touch or smell teaches us about our universe. We need not to contemplate or ask questions. Our sensory organs report to our brains, and our brains interpret the data and send the report to our hearts. So, if we see a loving smile, hear loving words or feel a loving touch, the brain processes this information and concludes, "Hey, we are being loved right now!" When we are loved, there is tangible proof. It's not an abstract thought or feeling, it is concrete and evidenced. As King Solomon wrote in his book of Proverbs (27:19), "As water reflects a man's face back to him, so is the heart of one man to another." This means, when treated with love, your heart feels that love.

LOVE IS AN ACT

How do we know that we love someone? The answer is straightforward. When we behave lovingly towards someone, it means we love that person. When we ask a question like "What is love?" we assume that we're trying to define an abstract concept similar to "What is freedom?" or "What is good fortune?" But truthfully, love is not a concept. It's an act. Having to ask, "What is love?" is like asking, "What is running?" or "What is swimming?" If you've ever seen someone run or swim, you know what running and swimming entail. For love to be real, it must be expressed as an act.

AKNOWLEDGEMENTS

None of us got to where we are by ourselves. Whether the assistance we received was obvious or subtle, acknowledging someone's help is a big part of understanding the importance of saying thank you. I would like to thank God the Almighty for my life and all the trials and tribulations I have been through. I believe that for my age, I have endured a lot, but I blame no one for that but myself.

To all the girls I've loved before, thank you for the lessons of life. I couldn't have been who I am and where I am today if it was not for you. To KCRS FM, thank you TJ and David Malatsi for opening your hearts and home for mein the past 20 years and to your family, thank you guys. I have met many people along the way; famous people and not so famous people, who have played a role in my life, I thank you. If I can write your names it will be another book. So you know yourselves. To all my teachers in all the spheres of my education

Dankie, ngiyabonga for keeping up with me I know I was a headache. I have been to many Churches seeking God's face, and I forgot he is everywhere, Pastor Sakhile Sibiya and your wife, thanks baba and Pastor Abram Sibiya and Pastor Constance Sibiya. Mfundisi Nkosi at Siyabuswa of the Uniting Reformed Church, thanks for everything. Pastor Marry Mathibela, I know I have a lot to offer, thank you Victory Fellowship (Baba Tlou, Pastor Jabu Mahlangu and your wife) I thank God for you all in my life. You have planted a seed. To all my friends from Childhood, Facebook and instagram until now, you know yourselves, thank you. Vusi Nanas, you are special. The Mahlangu Family, my father's 20 kids, my sisters and my brothers … I love you. To one special Neighbour who took care of me, MaSkhosana and your family, I thank you. TB, R Boys, Musa, Thandeka, Sydney, MaB, Koketso. I wish my late grandmother was still alive, sad, only God knows. To my aunts, I love you and to my cousins, nephews and nieces, yhooo that's two pages of names, I love you. To my mother Thembane Rebecca Mbele, my prayer warrior, I love you so so much.

My sister Lindiwe and my little brother Vusiniyazi. How can I forget my elderly brother Fisi, you are my all. You know everything I went through in my life. Thank you for being the brother you are. Brian Temba cuz, Nhlanhla and Kiwi (Mama) thank you for your prayers. To my wife, my darling, Carol Makgabele Mbele. Thank you for understanding. I know I took a lot of your time writing this small book. We argued, but we agreed to disagree. This is a new page for us. I love you. To our little family Mom Girly, Karabo, Mahlatse, Katlego, Lindo, Mandisa, Nomfundo - they are just a handful. Sheila and Solly, we love you. To all my friend who contributed and motivated me, all friends following me on social media thank you, Thandekile Mokae, Thembi Makhaye, Tepza, Daniel Mokoena , Smanga Maphanga, Thulare, Thandi Modipela thank you so much. Shaka and Sesi my caterpillar. Thando Mahlangu, Siyathela. Ngiyathokoza wakwethu. Mzala Zodwa "aline Volo". Tshepo Gavu, I have so many problems baba. Bheki and Boitumelo Langa, TGC my inspiration. Vukulu Sizwe Maphindani, thank you for believing in me. Let's tell our story.

I have learned that life is beautiful, a struggle worth conquering, the world's not really against you. The only thing that's against you is yourself. I feel like everything in my life has led me to write this book. My choices, my heartbreaks, my regrets, everything, and when you read, my past seems worth it. Because if I had done one thing differently, I could have written the book earlier.

God causes things to happen at exactly the right time! Your job is not to figure out when, but to make up your mind that you won't give up until you cross the finish line and are living in the radical, outrageous blessings of God! The more you trust Jesus and keep your eyes focused on Him, the more life you'll have. Trusting God brings life. Believing brings rest. So stop trying to figure everything out, and let God be God in your life. Have you ever been in love? Horrible isn't it? It makes you so vulnerable. It opens your chest and it opens up your heart and it means that someone can get inside you and mess you up. You build up all these defenses, you build up a whole suit of armour, so that nothing can hurt you, then one stupid person, not different from any other stupid person, wanders into your life…

You give them a piece of you. They didn't ask for it. They did something dumb one day, like kiss you or smile at you, and then your life isn't your own anymore. Love takes hostages. It gets inside you. It eats you out and leaves you crying in the darkness as simple as a phrase like "maybe we should be friends" turns into a glass splinter working its way into your heart. It hurts. Not just the imagination. Not just the mind. It's a soul-hurt, it really gets-inside-you-and-rips-you-apart - pain. I hate love. They told you that beauty is in the eye of the beholder. What they failed to tell you is that it is best seen with the eyes closed. What you look like isn't important. What is important is who you are inside and the choices you are making in your life. Remember, our lives are storybooks that we write for ourselves; wonderfully illustrated by the people we meet.

This is my story.

With Love

Sipho Mbele

CONTENTS

PREFACE 1

AKNOWLEDGEMENTS 3

CHAPTER ONE: YESTERDAY, TODAY & TOMORROW 9

CHAPTER TWO: FRIENDS 13

CHAPTER THREE: BMD (BIRTHDAY, MARRIAGE & DIVORCE) 20

CHAPTER FOUR: THE AFTERMATH OF DIVORCE 27

CHAPTER FIVE: MY LESSONS ON MARRIAGE 32

CHAPTER SIX: WHAT MEN LOVE ABOUT WOMEN 38

CHAPTER SEVEN: WHAT MEN HATE ABOUT WOMEN 43

CHAPTER EIGHT: WE ARE DIFFERENT 52

CHAPTER NINE: MISUNDERSTANDING: SEX & RELATIONSHIP 55

CHAPTER TEN: YOU BELONG 81

CHAPTER TEN: TAKE IT FROM ME OR LEAVE 85

CHAPTER ELEVEN: CUT YOUR LOSSES 103

CHAPTER TWELVE: PATIENCE IS VIRTUE 119

CHAPTER THIRTEEN: WHY STAY? 122

CHAPTER FOURTEEN: GOD IS LOVE 127

CHAPTER FIFTEEN: FINITO 134

ABOUT THE AUTHOR 137

CHAPTER ONE
YESTERDAY, TODAY & TOMORROW

Growing up; no one ever told and taught me how to love and what love is. I don't want to say growing up was arduous, but it was fun and a learning curve. I was brought up by my grandmother in a small village in Mpumalanga, the then Kwandebele Homeland, where I became a centre of attraction in my family and the community.

Growing up in a big family was not what I anticipated and out of all my brothers, sisters and cousins, I think I had that attraction to fame and stardom. I remember when I was at primary school, I think I was at Standard 5 (Today's Grade 7); I had this girlfriend who was beautiful, clean and intelligent. At that age, I believed that she would be my wife. We were never in the same class, so communication was during breaks and through letters. In those days, when we wrote a letter it would be like this:

The silver cup is broken

No one can mend by you and me baby.

Dear Sma,

See you after school my baby, I love you and I can't wait to carry your books.

Yours Forever

Sipho Mbele

But something wrong happened on that day, the so-called "iposi" (Postman) whom was delivering the letter, was caught by the teacher, as he delivers the letter. You were in trouble when you had an affair at school in those days, and the punishment would be to tell your parents or read the letter out loud, holding hands in all senior classes - we chose the latter. It was fun, yet for me that's when I learned there is a thing called love. Well it ended with that girl as we grew up; I sometimes meet her from time to time. I grew up to be recognized and sometimes referred to as the ladies' man. I didn't know what I was doing, but it was fun. I remember having a string of girls, some fighting over me and by then, I thought I was the man. When I finished my matric I became a private teacher for a year, and life was about having someone to love and have fun with, even though I didn't understand what love is. I had an affair with one of the most beautiful teacher, whom I later discovered that she passed away.

May her soul rest in peace. She taught me how to kiss, and be a good lover. I was still young by then, maybe in my early 20s. Remember, I was the jack-of-all-trades; a dancer, singer, speaker and well a charmer. I was teaching ballroom dance to some community members, young and old. Initially I said, there is no one who ever taught me how to love and what love is. I met this woman, beautiful and she took my breath away, I don't know if I could say it was a problem or a blessing. She was 10 years older than me. But because I believe in our love; she therefore swept off my feet, and we fell in love. Maybe today I would be called a Ben 10, with all the criticism at that time; we cared little because we were in love. Thembi was the woman for me.

My family was against the relationship, society beheld me with rejection, but love conquers all, we didn't care. I had support from a friend called Mjasten who insisted that I go for initiation so that I can be a man and get circumcised. She was working for the government and I decided to go to university. Less I forget, she was divorced and didn't have children, and I didn't know that she would make me a man.

Oh! I didn't tell you, I was also seeing someone else at the time - Lindiwe, but she was not staying around; she would only come and visit during school holidays; and well, we were of the same age. Since I thought the world revolves around me, I impregnated Lindiwe, and in 6 months' time, I also impregnated Thembi, the older woman (I apologize for calling her that way). At a very young age, I had two kids who are grown women today, and whom I love dearly. What you didn't ask, Lindiwe told me she was pregnant but vanished and I was left with my Thembi who didn't know about the visitor , but the visitor knew about her. Since Lindiwe vanished, she never told me when she gave birth, I was always there for Thembi and the baby and I only knew her as my first-born child. I was angry that Lindiwe never told me about the baby and our relationship has been sour for both me and my daughter, until this day.

CHAPTER TWO

FRIENDS

There's a saying that goes, "birds of the same feathers flock together." Who didn't have one, who doesn't want friends? To tell you the truth, I had many people I knew and around me, but I had a music group called or named Shibarocksy (Shiba, Roni, Skhumbuzo and Sydney, that's me) that group was so powerful that, we actually used it as I vehicle through women. I was the champ there; well Skhumbuzo was worse with the underground movers Shiba and Roni. We were later joined by Poplar, who was also a "ladies man." These are the guys that will talk some sense to my head, to at least reduce the number of ladies I was involved with. Roni would say; "Starkato… relax baba."

Those were the days, and the nicest thing about it is

that we still meet from time to time with the addition of Artwell who became the mini me. But he is grown now. I continued staying with Thembi, I even moved away from home to stay with her, because I believed that I was loved. We moved to the suburbs in a bond house, well, she was paying for it; remember I was just a student. Whilst our baby was growing to a beautiful girl, I had a part-time job as a radio presenter at a community radio, which I'm still working for till today for the past 20 years. I was doing radio and school. I became famous and tried to be a man, father and student simultaneously. I still had pressure back home, since my family didn't support me, well not all of them. At-least I had support from some of my sisters and my elder brother. I didn't share this with anyone, but she was hard on me. I had to look after our baby, whilst she was working and paying attention to books. It was difficult, yet meanwhile I learned a lot, things like cooking, changing nappies and cleaning. I am grateful for those lessons, even thou those years I thought she didn't love me, but treating me as a younger brother. Well since the heart wants what it wants, whilst I was still with Thembi, I met this young beautiful Ndebele girl, who used to work at some retail stores at a new shopping centre that was opened around then, her name was Sbongile. She was quite, reserved and loving, and almost my age. Whilst things were not good at home, Thembi's family didn't support our relationship, she got pregnant with our second baby. I didn't tell you, at some point, I felt as if she cheated on me. But because I was young and gullible and was doing my things on the side I cared little, but it later hurt and haunted me that I didn't stood my ground with her. Well, I had my Sbongile then, what I didn't know was that she was a student at some University in the Western Cape, so that meant that she was working part time and as soon as the school reopens, she would leave back to school. We had fun; we would hold hands, kiss and walk in the rain. For us that was true love. I remember the radio station took me to Cape Town for a broadcasting course; there I met one friendly gentleman Siviwe, who later took me to the University of Cape Town so I can see Sbongile. She was happy to see me and I guess after that visit we lost contact as letter writing was the only means of communication. We later met in our adult lives and we became best of friends, she is happily married, so am I.

I returned from Cape Town, back to my life with Thembi and our kids. We had friends like black Sam Fana Mathebula, the late Lindiwe, well I can't discuss or write about them since this is about me. Well my relationship was the talk of the town, and remember I was studying also at Vista University, Mamelodi campus, doing BA Public Administration. I was doing well and a family man at that young age, until I met this woman…she was younger than me, beautiful, tough as she was doing aerobics and very clever. She was on demand, even my brother's friends wanted her, well since I had good moves, I got her first. Don't get me wrong, not that I still love her or want her, but truly, I was in love with Tshidi. We were inseparable, in the bus, at school. I remember in the cafeteria, we will go in holding hands. I remember a friend of mine Ditlaadi Sifike saying, 'That girl has bewitched you'. Today we laugh about it. Tshidi was the type of woman who was demanding attention, money, shopping, and I was a student, it was tough for me to maintain her but I tried. Well I did something that I identify as a wrong today, I introduced her to my elderly daughter who later gave away to her mother that she knows Tshidi and she was her mommy too. She was very loving, and I can tell you she is the only woman who slapped me, yes who slapped me, and I cried with one eye in the presence of my sisters.

Tshidi did something that I will never forget, I remember it was a Wednesday and I was writing MNA (Municipal Administration) paper. She was not writing, so I accompanied her to the main gate thinking she was taking a taxi home, only to find out that some boyfriend was waiting for her at the gate; her husband today, but hey, that's the interesting part, when she left me on that

Wednesday, the fool, who is me, didn't know that she was getting married on the very same Saturday. I was home on that Saturday and a friend of mine David, came and picked me up and said to me "baba, this, you have to see" we then drove to Tshidi's grandmothers' house, and I saw a big tent, I then asked my friend what was going on.

He said; I thought you knew, that your munch is getting married "I felt as if the whole world is crumbling on me. You know what was sad? One of my younger sisters knew about the wedding but she didn't bother to tell me. I felt so numb and I hated love for a second. How can a person I loved do this to me? Forgetting that I was doing the same thing to Thembi and my kids.

We then ended our relationship with Thembi and I lost Tshidi, who got married and I later found out that the husband was arrested and sent to prison. We tried again thereafter, but it was never the same. I even left University and got a job, to support my kids. I met Tshidi lately, she is grown, but she never apologized for hurting me, and I am asking myself, should she apologize?

Life is something else, I believe since then, my life became one mess after the other, and I met Thuli, who tried to commit suicide by drinking pills after I dumped her. I met Sesi who later died of heart congestion, whom today; her family claims I caused her death. I met Nomvula, whose father didn't like me, who later took us at gunpoint and asked us to end the affair. Remember I was now working, thanks to a friend Wendy who took me with to MTN 112 to work as a call Centre agent, where I met a lot of friends, abo Deli (very vocal), Felicia (my then crush, hope my wife won't kill me), Mduduzi, Thabo and this one woman who also hurt me, Sasa.

Sasa was also loving, but I must confess, I was a

player, yes I did love loved her, but my mind was all over the show. Whilst I was working for MTN after a year I decided it's time I go back to school and finish my studies. So I told my loving girlfriend I was going back to school. Guess what she said "you go back to school we done, I don't date school boys"I was hurt, but I left, because I had to fulfill my dreams and that was it for us.

I went back to TNG; I guess I was 30 years old when I took that decision. It was hard, but I had to do it. I remembered what my mother said to me "Sipho, God has formed and fashioned you for the plan and purpose he has for your life. As long as you doubt yourself, you will not attain the BEST God has for you. Bear in mind that God uses the foolish things of this world to confound the wise. God cannot use anything perfect because His strength is made perfect in our weakness. He does not call the qualified but qualifies the called. It does not matter what mess you're stuck in or have created, look to God and He will lift you up. Ask Him to help you see yourself as He sees you and all things will seem possible, doable and achievable." There and then I went back to school. Well I never took a break from relationships, even thou I was skeptical and my behaviour changed from then, I realized that love exists, but the problem was with me. I once claimed to love someone whom I didn't really know how to love. Sometimes we don't really love the person, we simply just hate being alone. The world had shut too many doors to my face, that the little attention she presented me with fooled both of us into believing it was love. I asked her out already knowing the answer to my request. I chased after her till she had said yes and there after she spent three years of her life chasing after me. She got tired, but see, I enjoyed having her chasing after me that at the thought of her leaving me, I falled fell to on my knees begging her to stay. She stayed, I made a promise that things will get better and I meant it, but the problem is I didn't know that to love her, I would first have to love myself. I didn't know that to love her I needed first to be comfortable with loving my broken self. So she gave me her heart and I broke it. I left her drowning in a pool of tears and I couldn't swim to save her because I was

CHAPTER THREE

BMD (BIRTHDAY, MARRIAGE & DIVORCE)

I Think in the trouble of finding myself and finding love, I forgot that God exist. I told you I was brought up by my grandmother, whom taught me how to pray the Lord's Prayer. Nani, as she is known to her kids, my aunts and uncles, the old lady who bought me my first keyboard. For whom my cousin Bongani believes she left me with charms when she passed on. My granny Mamorajane Nani Mbele was a God fearing woman, she instilled in me the instinct to pray and worship God, I will never forget her for that, well all this things of hurting and being hurt by love in case there's anything like that, was my own doing, I just forgot that too often we try to understand the journey, but life is meant to be lived not to be understood. You benchmark your progress against others' and pull yourself down, totally blind to the reality that everyone is on their own journey, walking their own unique path. No two destinies are exactly the same.

Think about making popcorn. You put in all the popcorn seeds in the boiling oil at the same time, the oil is exactly equal in temperature, but the popcorn do not all pop at the same time. Even identical twins who attend the same schools, with the same teachers, take the same course at University, go to the same classes and graduate on the same day, will not get a job on the same day. Jesus Christ was trained and prepared for his life purpose for thirty years, Joseph was in training for seventeen years, and Moses took forty years, what about Job? Yet we do not see them praying prayers that will break the spirit of delay, or commanding the death of stagnation nor praying against the spirit of slow progress in their lives. Do not undermine God's season of preparation in your life. Do not overlook the value of training.

Understand your purpose in life, accept the season of preparation and training, do not rush ahead of God and want to do and accomplish things before your set time. There is a set season for every purpose under the sun. Anything you do in your own strength ahead of its time is not sustainable; allow God to perfect all that concerns you and be willing to wait because the plan is with Him. His plan for your life is complete, it is perfect and it lacks nothing. Live no one else's life or adopt someone else's reality. Stay in your lane and let God do what He planned for you before the foundation stones of the earth. Be open to His direction and leadership, sometimes the answer is yes, sometimes the answer is no and other times it is wait. Wait upon the Lord and stop trading in your purpose by trying to live up to the expectation of others. You are original and unique, not a photocopy or a duplicate of the original, there is only one you and that you is a treasure in God's hands. Stay true to your life purpose and calling: Remain in the hold of your Creator. Do not limit what God can do through you because you doubt yourself. Someone sees a hero in you, someone sees royalty in you, someone sees and feels hope in you. Arise out of the pit of hopelessness and self-destruction, God holds better tomorrows for you. I just realized that my life was just beginning.

I thought I was done and I have done it all, but never realized that the best was yet to come. After completing my studies, I met a Dr, who later played a pivotal role within my family, by giving medical treatment, which saved a life. I will forever be grateful to her. You know in the mist of all the things I went through in my life, I have learnt that people come for a reason in your life and God will remove them when their season is done, and that's how I will forever look at that relationship with the good doctor in my life. There was one of the top muso and actress and politicians in the country, who came and go after the purposes was served. Please as you read here, don't get me wrong I have been hurt and I have hurt people too in my life, but I take that as a learning curve, I have forgiven them and I hope they have, if they haven't, I am sorry there's nothing I can do, only God knows. Then I was I was Married…. Oh no…what was I thinking. This is the part of my life that prompted me to write this book, Bongiwe and Tana will be my witnesses to what I endured in my marriage. The reason why I want you, yes you are reading to understand what every man wants from a woman. Women likes to say that all men are dogs, yet they do not know nor understand the reasons that will prompt men to behave in a certain manner.

Then I was married, and then I was divorced. Don't get me wrong she was beautiful; I did something that I can't even explain. We met, and in 6 weeks - we were married. I am so embarrassed to talk about this. I didn't pay lobola, I don't even know her family, we just got married, I didn't even tell my family, only my sister knew, because she was my witness, with my friend Sydney, Dali, Bucks Gamela, Zanele, Kindjie and adluphuthu. And I got married the day we signed, that's the day I was also burying my Uncle Morris. Oh! I don't know if it was a curse or what, that woman was mean, rude and unloving, but I was married. And I strongly believe that she is the reason I am sharing my life story with you. Through all this I learned that money can't buy you love. I had everything you can imagine of, but I was never happy. The end result was a divorce. I remember a friend named Kgomotso, who was going through the same thing, consoled me and we shared ideas on how we were going to go through this. I think my divorce came first and hers after. I was alone at the court; my wife soon to be ex, didn't come.

On the papers I said I wanted nothing since all we had was almost hers, maybe I was scared, I gave up R3 million in settlement. I just wanted my freedom and maybe to take some time off love and its shenanigans. At some point I wished that my mother (Ausi Ribs) would say this to me, when I told her I was getting married:

"lalela kahle Sipho wam, you are now a man. Tomorrow you will have a new mother, a new cook and a new person to share all your secrets with. It will no longer be me but her. Love your new mom even more than you love me. Before you walk into her arms forever, let me give you some words to guide you.

There was a day I was arguing with your father we were screaming, tempers were high. I was angry and he was angry too, then I called him an idiot! He was shocked. He looked at me asking how dare I called him that, immediately I Started calling him an idiot, fool, stupid, crazy. I called him all sorts of names, and guess what he did? He didn't raise his hands to hit me; he just walked away, bangs the door as he went out.

My Son, If your father had hit me and destroyed my eyes, how will you feel sitting here with me today? How will you regard him as your father? Would you have been proud of him or would you be blaming me for calling him names? Never hit your wife! No matter the provocation just walk away and things will be normal. Whenever she offends you, think of this story I just told you, it could have been your mom! Before I forget, after he left, I was filled with guilt. We slept on the same bed that night and I went to him the next day. I pleaded with him, I did all I could to show how sorry I am and he forgave me. That day I cooked his favorite meal; yes you know he loves mala mogodu right?

After that day, I never called him names; my respect for him was ten times stronger. There is something very important that you must always do, my son listen very carefully, defend your wife. When she is under pressure, stand by her. If your friends hate her, it is your duty to make them see her as a Queen. Your Uncle, I mean Uncle Jabu, never liked me. But your father was always supportive until his perception changed. There was a day your Father would host his friends. They were three . In that day I was in the kitchen, cooking for them and your father went to buy drinks. When the table was set and food was served. Everyone started eating. Then I remembered I did not add salt in the food. I was embarrassed. Your father tasted the food and looked at me. He immediately turned to the guests. He told them he instructed his wife last month not to add salt whenever she is cooking because of some problem with his body. He said it in a funny way and everyone laughed! The guests understood and he asked me to bring salt and everyone added according to their taste. He managed to eat the food without salt. After the guest left, he went on his knees and asked God to forgive him for lying.

Your wife is like a baby, sometimes she don't know what to say or do. Stand up and speak for her!

Now let me talk to you about sex. You see, sex is a wonderful thing. Do not be surprised if your wife enjoy and need sex more than you do. There were days I needed sex more than your father and there were days he needed it more than me but the important thing is to always try to satisfy the other when they need you. Don't always think of yourself. There was a time when things were hard and I needed to do two jobs to support your father. One night I was so tired. When I got to bed he was in the mood. He tried to make love to me and I didn't refuse him. I was tired but I felt I needed to be there when he needed me. When he tried undressing me, he saw my look and he stopped. He asked what was wrong and I said nothing. But he understands me better. He then stopped and then told me stories until I fell asleep. My son, Sex is best enjoyed when the two parties are physically and mentally ready for it. Sometimes, read your wife and understand her. Make it a habit to go anywhere with your wife. Besides work, move around with her. If anyone invite you to his house and told you not to come with your wife then be very careful. Use wisdom. I know you love m. I know you tell me all your problems. But now things will be different. Let your wife be the first to know before me. Let her be the first to see before me. When you have problems with her don't run to me immediately. Wait for a day to pass and then talk to her about it. Pray about it. Finally, don't forget to come and visit me with your wife every month!

I know you will have a happy home. You will always be my boy.

CHAPTER FOUR

THE AFTERMATH OF DIVORCE

I Tried finding a simple definition of a divorce, and I couldn't, but this came to mind, "marriage has gone wrong, the end. "I was divorced, I think after four years in the wilderness. I vowed, never to get married again, and guess what, I was wrong. I am going to share the lessons I learnt, the hard way of course. These are lessons I learnt too late. But these are lessons I am learning and committed in carrying forward. Truth is, I loved being married, and in time, I got married again and I am going to build my marriage with a foundation that will endure any storm and any amount of time.

If you are reading this and finding wisdom in my pain, share it with young men whose hearts are still full of hope, and with those you may know who may have forgotten how to love. One of those men may be like I was, and in these hard earned lessons perhaps something will awaken in him and he will learn to be the man his lady has been waiting for.

MEN- THIS IS YOUR CHARGE: Commit to being an EPIC LOVER. There is no greater challenge, and no greater prize. Your woman deserves that from you. Be the type of husband your wife can't help but brag about. There is hope. Others will say, (marriage is nie pap and melk) well take it from me, it's all up to you to make it work. I am writing this book, I am married again and happy. I didn't give up on love. She is actually here next to me on Facebook. Love is the message and the message is love.

My advice to men after a divorce or break-up. Obviously, I'm not a relationship expert. But there's something I learnt about love through my divorce.

- Fall in love over and over again. You will constantly change. In years you will not be the same person you are today. Change will come, and in that you have to re-choose each other every day. SHE DOESN'T HAVE TO STAY WITH YOU, and if you don't take care of her heart, she may give that heart to someone else or seal you out completely, and you may never get it back. Always fight to win her love just as you did when you were courting her.

- Protect your own heart. Just as you committed to being the protector of her heart, you must guard your own with the same vigilance. Love yourself fully, love the world openly, but there is a special place in your heart where no one must enter except for your wife. Keep that space always ready to receive her and invite her in, and refuse to let anyone or anything else enter there.

- Never stop courting. Never stop dating. NEVER EVER take that woman for granted. When you asked her to marry you, you promised to be that man that would OWN HER HEART and to fiercely protect it. This is the most important and sacred treasure you will ever be entrusted with. SHE CHOSE YOU. Never forget that, and NEVER GET LAZY in your love.

- Never blame your woman if you get frustrated or angry at her, it is only because it is triggering something inside of YOU. They are YOUR emotions, and your responsibility. When you feel those feelings take time to get present and to look within and understand what is it inside of YOU that is asking to be healed. You were attracted to this woman because she was the person best suited to trigger all of your childhood wounds in the most painful way so you could heal them… when you heal yourself, you will no longer be triggered by her, and you will wonder why you ever were.

- Allow your woman to just be. When she's sad or upset, it's not your job to fix it, it's your job to HOLD HER and let her know it's ok. Let her know that you hear her, and that she's important and that you are that pillar on which she can always lean. The feminine spirit is about change and emotion and like a storm her emotions will roll in and out, and as you remain strong and unjudging she will trust you and open her soul to you... DON'T RUN-AWAY WHEN SHE'S UPSET. Stand present and strong and let her know you aren't going anywhere. Listen to what she is really saying behind the words and emotion.

- Be willing to take her sexually, to carry her away in the power of your masculine presence, to consume her and devour her with your strength, and to penetrate her to the deepest levels of her soul. Let her melt into her feminine softness as she knows she can trust you fully.

- Give her space... The woman is so good at giving and giving, and sometimes she will need to be reminded to take time to nurture herself. Sometimes she will need to fly from your branches to go and find what feeds her soul, and if you give her that space she will come back with new songs to sing.... (okay, getting a little too poetic here, but you get the point. Tell her to take time for herself, ESPECIALLY after you have kids. She needs that space to renew and get re-centred, and to find herself after she gets lost in serving you, the kids and the world.)

- It's not your job to change or fix her... your job is to love her as she is with no expectation of her ever changing. And if she changes, love what she becomes, whether it's what you wanted or not.

- Take full accountability for your own emotions: It's not her job to make you happy, and she CAN'T make you sad. You are responsible for finding your own happiness, and through that your joy will spill over into your relationship and your love. There are times were you need to be silly. Don't take yourself so damn seriously. Laugh. And make her laugh. Laughter makes everything else easier.

CHAPTER FIVE

MY LESSONS ON MARRIAGE

I Have said a lot about myself and the women I have dated. I have seek God's face and asked for forgiveness for all my trespasses and to all the people I have wronged. It's time I reflect about what I have learnt in my journey. Don't get me wrong; I am happy, content and married as I write this book. Married to a beautiful woman, Makgabele, intelligent, and full of wisdom. She is sometimes referred to as a career woman. I have known her for many years as her mother, my now mother in-law was my High school teacher and she knows half of my messy life. I love my wife and we are always trying to follow these simple rules of do's and don'ts.

Often a lot is shared about what women hate or love about men. I have decided to be real and share with women, from a men's perspective what men love and hate about women. Read and learn. I shared a quotation with a friend of mine Thandi Modibela, "if he's mad brush his head and kiss him." And guess what? Her response was, "will African man approve?" I've come to notice that most women or men do not know nor understand why men are the way they are when it comes to the emotion we call love.

As a young man you are told to "man up", "don't be no chicken", and "stop complaining" because we (as men) are supposed to be the strength and the backbone of the family, and you can't do that as some emotional dude. So we are raised with the thought that showing emotion is weakness, and you're less of a man if you do it. This is compared to women, who are taught that because they are women, they have every right to be emotional, and that it's okay to cry and be upset. The only emotions most men have growing up are anger and happiness. We are forced to bottle up our sadness and compassion. Emotions like love and affection are very foreign to us, especially with females. The only female we have those sort sorts of feelings for from the jump is our mothers. That's because it's ok and its acceptable at that time, hence the reason we look for our women in the image of our mothers. Now this is a double-edged sword because it causes us to have very high standards, this can scare females away if they feel they can't measure up.

When we actually tune these emotions of love and

affection for another woman, it's fairly new. We don't know how to act and we go all out. That's why that first heartbreak is the only heartbreak it takes to turn a man bad. We actually open up 100%, tell you how we really feel, holding hands, all which seems like cool stuff. Then the unthinkable happen - heartbreak. So the thought process now is why would I open up to a chick ever again. I was always told to bottle my emotions up. I'm going back to that. To resort to this doesn't make a man weak at all, it's just how we were brought up in society. This is in comparison to women, who can honestly fall in love in their younger years. They are more familiar with these feelings and how to deal with them. Women will have multiple heartbreaks, but in all honesty, a man will probably get his heartbroken once, maybe twice. That's how real it is.

What women must understand is that when a man loves, he loves hard. That's all we know how to do. Dudes don't get in a relationship to kill time or just because it's what he's used to. A man gets in a relationship because those feelings are genuine. Men "just want to hump everything" it's not always the answer to why we are sometimes scared of commitment and relationships. It's actually the fear of you wanting a relationship just to have one, you switching up as time goes on, and then us being hurt again. A hurt man is very hard to get to. We have reverted back to not showing emotion, which causes women to feel that all men are cold hearted and don't care. That isn't the case. We just don't know how to handle being vulnerable at the end of the day, especially when good men are always overlooked because most women want this "tough guy", not one who's "too soft". Women even go as far as to call men who show emotion "stupid and sissy". It's understood that you always have to be a man about your business regardless, but it's still frowned upon later on in life to open up too much. The problem is most men don't know how to balance showing just enough emotion. It's either showing none or showing all.

For those who have read all of this and still don't understand where I'm coming from, let me simplify this. As a man, our first interaction with a woman is with our mother. It is the deepest love there is, unconditional love. Therefore, when we are introduced to love in the sense of a relationship, we fall and we fall hard, and when that doesn't work we're hurt. Love is a foreign subject to men. We don't know how to handle it because we weren't taught about it from our early years. Heartbreak or the pain that comes from a failed relationship is something that we honestly can't handle emotionally. We haven't been able to learn what these emotions really mean. As we get older we realize what love really is, and how to go about it the appropriate way. My advice to men is this. It's okay to have emotions. Just know where and when not to show them. No woman wants a man whose barriers are up 24/7. Part of growing up is getting over the past.

Getting hurt is going to happen. Sometimes we end up overlooking overlook a good woman holding on to past relationships. If you feel some type of way gents, it's okay to speak on it. You're supposed to, but remember that you have to do it in moderation and when it actually matters. You can't complain and nitpick at the things females do because at the end of the day, you're a man regardless. Just as there's a double standard concerning sex for women, there is always going to be will always be a double standard attached to the emotions of men that we have to live with. My advice to women. If you have a good man who does open up and show you love, don't look down on him. A lot of women tend to poke fun at guys who aren't scared to show their emotions. It doesn't make us "sissies", it makes us human. I had trouble writing this in fear that people would be like "who hurt you?" until I realized I don't really care what people think. Everyone's been hurt before and every male can relate to this. You have to be real with yourself. I'm someone who handles and understands emotion very well due to experience. I've had those problems showing emotion after the first heartbreak, so I've been through it. You live and you learn! This is the everyday struggle men face out here!! It's too real. Now you know why most of us are the way we are. Getting hurt isn't what men want, or even can, handle. So this is why we're extra selective when it comes to whom with whom we deal with on that type of level. Is it a good thing or bad thing??? Hmm.

CHAPTER SIX

WHAT MEN LOVE ABOUT WOMEN

KNOW YOUR MAN

How often do you feel that a man has drifted away from you saying, "Lebo doesn't understand me". Don't let him go there, understand him. Love can only grow and deepen through understanding. You can never get to the point where you think you know everything about him. You may think a man is simple; in fact he is a complex person that even he doesn't understand. You need to love him and get to know him with patience and determination; this is a key on to how to love a man better.

WE LOVE IT WHEN YOU LISTEN TO US

In many instance women complain about guys who don't listen when they talk, same goes for us. We also notice when you give us the duuh at whatever moment and when you are not interested in what we say. If we notice that you are tired, we can keep it short and to the point, at least try to listen though.

WE LOVE A STRONG WILL WOMAN

Women have this perception that men love a less talker, no ways. Men love a woman that can be talked into anything. We like a challenge. We also like it when you have an opinion on something. Even if you don't agree don't be afraid to voice it out. Actually, that's how good conversations take place. Men like challenges, so talk sister and challenge him.

RANDOMLY TEXT OR CALL US

Men also love it when you randomly call or just send a hello text. We are not the ones who are supposed to show that we are thinking about you, let us know that you are thinking about us. We like the things said or texted. Guys love that. Women wait for men to text first, they always respond.

THAT SMELL

Guys love a woman who smells good. No matter how you look, if you have that intoxicating smell, we stick to you like glue. We will tolerate more than usual, just because of that smell. Not a whole lot but enough to leave that scent when you hug us or smack us, well, depending on the situation.

GETTING OUT OF THE SHOWER/BATH

A man loves it when a woman gets out of the shower or bath. There is nothing sexier than a woman who is just out of the shower, either in a robe, towel or eeeeh nothing. And sure some women don't want to be pounced and sexed up as soon as they clean off, but we need not to have sex. But some TLC's will be pretty damn cool.

GIVE HIM SPACE

Whilst a woman often needs attention, a man needs space and time. Men thrive on being focused on and directed, and sometimes they need to clear their minds to focus on what is important to them at that moment. Accept it -may not be you. It's important to give him time to respond to a situation. Women often respond immediately, instinctively, but a man can take more time, to reflect and formulate a response. Understand this and give him time, don't jump into conclusions. There are times, also, when men need space just to be... well, nothing. Men thrive on periods of emptiness, allow them that. Get this right and you will really know how to love a man.

BE HONEST

We love it when you are honest with us. Yebo, even if it's something bad, guys are all about a woman who tells the truth. Even if it's cheating, we atleast have some respect left if you're just upfront about it. Honesty is the best policy for guys. We hate finding out stuff by ourselves and trust me - we don't forgive easily. We love itwhen you are upfront with us. We don't like vague answers, like maybe, eish, and writing down on the ground or biting your nails. A girl will know the first time if they want to date a guy or not. So don't fear hurting us.

SHOW AFFECTION

We love it when you're affectionate. Guys like attention, but we particularly like being touched by you. You can strike and brush my head.

MAKE US FEEL AMAZING

Men need to feel good about themselves and often don't. They may live in their power but not be convinced by it. Make him feel he deserves it; make him realizes that he is the man he would like to be. It's important to do this from a genuine appreciation of him and his qualities. He should believe what you say otherwise everything disappears. Inspire him to be more of himself. You have to understand this to know how to love a man. These are just a few things that men love. Let's check the opposite end of the spectrum.

CHAPTER SEVEN

WHAT MEN HATE ABOUT WOMEN

Eish, this is a one difficult part, where a lot of my brothers will think I am dishing out our secrets to women. Sorry guys, just schooling them about what we don't like about them.

DON'T ASK WHERE I AM

Ladies, men hate it when you call them and ask where they are. It feels like you monitoring and spying on them, its annoying.it feels like you treating him like a baby. Stop it, it's boring.

JUMPING INTO CONCLUSIONS

We hate it when you jump into conclusions. Now, I know it sounds like we may do the same thing when talking about your ex a sexy hunk co-worker, but we never voice those opinions unless we have A reason to think something may actually be going on. But, when were on Facebook and you notice a chick I used to go to school with that has a husband and three kids poked me and you go apeshit…that not good. Or you see a lipstick on my cheek and smack the hell out of me. Understandable …unless I ran into my grandma who wears too much lipstick and you didn't give me time to explain. That's not on, you don't have a right to slap me as I don't have one either.

DON'T COMPARE US

Guys hate it when you compare them to your old flame or another guy. When we do something stupid, don't say, "Sfiso never does that. He's always getting his girlfriend shoes. "Well if Sfiso is so damn awesome, dress up sexy and have him get the shoes. If we do something stupid or that aggravates you, just tell us that it's stupid and aggravating and that would be enough. Telling us that Jabu, the hunky intern always calls his girlfriend even if he's busy makes us want to not call you even more, it'll backfire, so be careful. We don't mind mentioning how Thabo dances. However when you mention how Tsepho looked like a stud in his new outfit today or that your ex called and you talked and talked, we get peeved. We don't mind competition, but don't want to be paranoid that you're getting some on the side either. If you talk about stuff like that, reassures us that we're still the 'bees knees' in your eyes.

DON'T MOTHERS US

Men often retain a bond with their mother and like to be looked after by them. Don't drift into being his mother or try to supersede her. He needs you as a lover. Women can end up just taking care of their man and men accept this. This is potentially disastrous. He doesn't really want this from you. This is especially true after you have children. Take care you still treat him as your lover; this will be what he is missing.

DON'T INSULT US

We hate it when you insult us, even as a joke. When we're the butt of a joke you tell in front of your friends or family, it doesn't sit well with us. Makes us feel inferior and stupid. Unless we agree it's ridiculous, try to steer clear of mentioning us doing anything embarrassing, shameful, stupid, or weird. If you have second thoughts about saying something, chances are, we don't want you to say it.

WE HATE DRAMA

We hate it when you're dramatic just to get attention. Guys can't stand drama in any shape or form. If you do it consistently, we'll move on. We don't care if you're Mkabayi or Thandaza, we HATE drama. Period. Especially drama over something that's so trivial, we can't fathom why it bothers you.

SELFISHNESS

We hate it when you are selfish. Selfishness is a major turn off. Only thinking of yourself and not being considerate of others is something that many guys won't tolerate. Like being obnoxious when drunk or using foul language around my Christian friends or family. Be considerate of your surroundings. Don't be selfish.

UNHYGIENIC

We hate it when you're not hygienic. Nothing turns a guy off more than smelling funky, looking funky, or both. We understand that you work out...but not sitting around for four hours in your own sweat, then wanting us to have sex with you. And then getting mad when we suggest a shower first. It's common courtesy. If you want us to go downtown, make sure downtown's neatly trimmed and has no awkward smells. We don't obsess over it, but if you think it may smell bad, you may need to do a quick check up. We won't mind.

EMPTY PROMISES

We hate it when you break promises. Guys don't like to be let down that much. Sometimes it can't be helped, but it doesn't change us not liking it. If you can't make it to something or will be real late, simply let us know. Or if you even THINK something may come up, don't make a 100 percent promise to make it. Simply tell us you'll try your best or do what you can, but can't make any guarantees. We'll appreciate that and won't have high expectations.

WE HATE SHOPPING.

We hate it when you drag us to shopping. Men and women's minds are weird when it comes to shopping. To have peace and a great day, don't take us to Woollies or Mary's fashion, go there by yourself. Men rarely spend hours deciding on colour, comparison shopping or finding the sale prices. We know what we want; we get in, buy our shirt, and get out. 10-15 minutes and we're done. Mission accomplished.

With women, the trying on of garments takes a long time. Not sure why. I know if Carol goes into the dressing room, I won't see her again for the next 20-30 minutes. I sit there waiting patiently, contemplating the meaning of life or if I should just end mine right now. Then, she'll say nothing fits just right. Or the colour wasn't right. Or, "It makes me look fat." On a funny note, men also hate it when you destruct them watching their favourite sport.

WATCHING FOOTBALL WITH A WOMAN IS REALLY STRESSFUL:

Wife: Honey which teams are playing?

Husband: Arsenal vs Manchester United.

Wife: Oooh wonderful! I Love Arsenal..

Husband: That's a good team.

Wife: Is Drogba playing?

Husband: He doesn't play for any of these teams...

Wife: Okay sweeety. Is that Chris Brown?

Husband: [bored] No he is Chamberlain.

Wife: Okay but they look the same. What's that yellow card for?

Husband: It's a Warning to the Player.

[After few minutes Rooney scores for Manchester United]

Wife: [cerebrates in high mood] Is that Chamberlain who has scored?

Husband: [calmly] No it's Rooney for Manchester United!

Wife: [furious] How? it should be arsenal who should have scored!!

Husband: [silent]

Wife: What is that Red card for?

Husband: [bored] That means the player should go out of the pitch for misbehaving.

Wife: Then is he going to be a Coach?

Husband: [unwilling to answer] Aaaaaaaaa no...

Wife: It's the same with Traffic Lights: Yellow=Warning; Red=Danger.

Husband: Exactly darling...

Wife: What about the Green Card?

Husband: Mmmm nothing of that kind in a field of play....

Wife: I want Arsenal to win the World Cup...

Husband: [silent]

Wife: Who is that man standing who looks like Mr. Bean?

Husband: [bored] it's the Arsenal coach, Arsene Wenger.

Wife: that means the other opponent's coach is Manchester Wenger?

Husband: [CHANGES THE CHANNEL]

CHAPTER EIGHT

WE ARE DIFFERENT

Men show their love differently than women. Men tend to believe that they are showing their love by doing things for and with their partners. These include financially supporting a woman, spending time with her, going for a walk, watching TV, going to a restaurant, getting the car fixed and having sex. This kind of love is called. "Shared activity". A man shows his love by spending time with his partner and doing things with her. Words are unnecessary.

Women, on the other hand, show their love by discussion and personal sharing. This is the kind of thing women do with each other. There is a heavy emphasis on verbal communication. Emotional intimacy is the main theme. Love is demonstrated by being honest about feelings, being open and talking about the relationship.

Women appreciate men who can occasionally talk

about their feelings and be open and vulnerable. If you're feeling anxious about sex or concerned about an erection, why not say so? If you appreciate her in some special way, why not say that too? Women also want a man who can say, "Honey, I love you". No chronic illnesses prevent a man from pleasing their partner in this important way. Men simply don't realize how important it is to say these words. Men relate physically and women relate emotionally. Stop and think for a moment how society has taught men to relate to each other. They shake hands, slap each other on the back and hug one another. Men give "bear hugs" to each other on important occasions. A father and son relate by wrestling. Men and boys do things together. They play ball, tackle each other and play soccer on Saturday mornings. For men, words have nothing to do with relating. Action is the name of the game. This is one reason why a sexual problem can be so difficult for guys. Society hasn't taught men on how to talk about these issues. Embarrassment often prevents verbal communication. Not surprisingly, women have been socialized to relate with words. Women feel there is hope for a relationship to the extent that the couple can talk about problems. Most women don't enjoy talking about cars, sports or things of interest to men. They feel cared for if they are complimented, appreciated and romanced in soft, loving kinds of ways. Women like to be told that they look nice or that their assistance is appreciated. Men often take these things for granted and see a little need to go into such details.

They feel that women should just "know" these things and that saying them is unnecessary. Why waste words? In summary, men and women are different in more ways than the obvious. Women want a man who can be genuine, open, honest and considerate. This doesn't come easily for most men. It takes real effort to stay present, be emotionally available and sensitive to the needs of one's partner. By focusing less on the physical issues however, a couple can often achieve a new level of closeness and intimacy.

CHAPTER NINE

MISUNDERSTANDING: SEX & RELATIONSHIP

There are always exceptions and we are not attempting to introduce any hard, fast rules but I do believe that we can make some very safe assumptions. With relationships men are normally a lot more casual in their thinking than women. Women usually tend to want a serious relationship. Most women are taught to look for a strong male figure for leadership and support. The average woman wants to have stability in their interpersonal relationships. She does not want to have sex partners for the sake of sex only. Sex is a more sacred thing to most women probably because she is the receiver during sexual intercourse. Women tend to be more emotional so a woman will be led by her heart more than her head which is fine because she is a compliment to a man. Men and women are wired differently because they were designed by God to compliment each other in a relationship. A woman may notice positive re-actions from a man as a sign of commitment when they may not necessarily be so. Positive re-actions on his part are definite signs of interest but not commitment. A man may be just feeling the relationship out. He may or may not notice signs of the relationship lasting longer but men are typically very slow to commit to any permanent relationship.

In his unconscious mind a woman must pass a series of tests before he will even consider a long-term relationship. Once a woman sees what she discerns to be positive signs, she may assume that a man is actually beginning the process of a long-term relationship in his mind. She may become more demanding in the way that she deals with him because she is expecting him to behave as though he is in a permanent relationship. A man may pick up on this and wonder what happened to the woman he met. This may give him a negative reflection of what the relationship is supposed to be. This is the time when he will typically bail out of the relationship, which often leaves a woman wondering what happened. One mistake that many women will often make is to think that a man perceives sex as commitment.

In her mind, sex may hold a place of value because she values her body but this is not necessarily how a man perceives it. He will probably view sex as just having a good time and not a tool that can be used to advance towards the next level in a relationship. This aspect of relationship alone seems to be the main paradox between men and women. Contrary to most's belief, if a man is serious - he will wait much enough before sex. Usually a woman believes that if she consents to sex with a man he will appreciate her more and want to be in an everlasting relationship. This may not be the case, and a man my loose respect based on such paradox of understanding.

One more mistake that many women seem to make is to broadcast their beautiful bodies. They will display their bodies like billboards. The message seems like this is what you get when you get me. Let me say these to all women: "that this is the biggest mistake that you can possibly make when it comes to men."

A man will always remember you based on the first

impression he gets from you. If you broadcast your body as a sex thing, that is the only impression he will ever have of you. Once that impression is made, there is absolutely nothing you can do to ever change it. A man is more impressed a clean woman, healthy, and well dressed. If he sees you as an intelligent sophisticated woman you will have a better chance of a long term relationship than if he perceives you as a sex object. There is more to love than sex.

CAN THABO AND NTOMBI BE FRIENDS?

One of the longest running debates amongst men and women is whether or not, straight men and women can ever be friends – that is to say, can a friendship exist without sexual or romantic attraction. In a few recent conversations I had with both my female and male friends about this debate, didn't get a satisfying answergot no satisfying answer. I had to rely on my perspective, from a man's point of view, and in my opinion, up to 95% of men, the answer is NO, not with my woman. The question that follows will be; who is it that you don't trust between the male friend and your own woman? Is this attraction and romance or just a friendship?

To start with: The fact that a man may be attracted to a woman – or believe that Busi's attracted to Thabo – automatically disqualifies a friendship and implies that ultimately it is his and only his view that defines "just friends". For another, the idea that just being attracted to somebody means that the relationship isn't "just" a friendship carries the implication that there is a magical dividing line between Romantic or sexual attraction and friendship. It's a sexy topic, rife with stereotypes and joking-but-not-really stereotypes about men and women and teasing the idea that your supposedly platonic friend is actually harboring a secret crush on you and whether this is a good or bad thing for the relationship. People who believe that yes, men and women can be friends without sex becoming a wedge will talk about their plethora of male or female friends with whom they share no romantic entanglements, while those who believe that they can't will cast aspersions on the male half of the pairing (and it's always men who are supposedly the weakest link in this equation) and insisting they would gladly bone the hell out of their girlfriends if given half a chance.

We love the idea that there's some sort of impossible wall between men and women and ascribe all sorts of motivations to it – that men only are friends with women because they want to sleep with them or that women know that their male friends want them and string them along because they enjoy the ego boost or because they get their jollies over the power they wield. libidos somehow make them unable to be friends with someone they find attractive, I believe that not only can men and women be "just" platonic friends… it's the obsession with the question that's the problem. The idea that men and women can't be "just" friends presume the fact that attraction means it is automatically unacknowledged… or that it will inevitably be enacted upon. Yet in the real world, friends can acknowledge attraction – whether one-sided or mutual – without destroying things. It's entirely possible for a couple to say "Yeah, we know it would never work out and we don't want to risk ruining our friendship with an ugly break-up". Men (or women) are quite capable of being attracted to each other and keeping that attraction to the realm of fantasy or "it would be fun if…"

without actively trying to pursue it. My final take after all the conversations I had is, Friendship – real friendship – can encompass sex or love without being "ruined", so long as everybody is honest with one another and willing to act like adults. The choice is yours, whether you want to have the type of friend in your relationship.

JEALOUSY MY SISTER, CONTROL IT.

In my past relationships, I encountered a lot of jealousy women. Some would wake up at night and open my phone to read my messages. Some would call the last number of the lady dialed on my phone, only to find out that it's a business call. The funny part, the last straw, was when I organized with a friend Bongi, to have her send me a message, that reads "thank you uncle bae, last night was good." And guess what, my ex-girlfriend was so furious, but the interesting part was, I was with her last night. And I dumped her.

Now my beautiful sister, you need to ask yourself,

is your jealousy tearing your relationship apart? Are you jealous of every person in your men's life that came before you? Do you have a hard time trusting your men because of your history of being betrayed? Don't let it threaten your future and your happiness. Ask yourself why you are choosing this behavior. Everybody has a way of being in the world. Is your way being jealous, accusatory, highly monitoring and smothering? Why are you choosing that? Is it because you have a history of being cheated on? There's an expression: "What I fear, I create." Are you testing your partner until he just finally fails? If you fear that somebody will cheat on you, you may just push him to a point where someone else may grab his attention. Imagine if someone else treated your Mandla with dignity and respect, didn't challenge his integrity every minute of every hour, but was in fact accepting, peaceful and harmonious. These really matter. You need to worry about what you're creating. Ask yourself: Are you responsible for the previous relationships in which you were betrayed? Did you run those previous partners off with your jealous behaviour?

Jealousy is a poorly disguised need for power and

control. Jealous people are tyrannical, controlling, domineering and completely insensitive to the impact of their actions on their partner. Are you getting a power trip off of this? Is the payoff that you keep your partner on a short leash and completely under your control?

Choose to respect your partner and make some different choices. You have more power in your love, respect, personality and magnetism than you do in control. You can't make him come home, but you can make him want to come home.

ADVICE FOR MEN ON JEALOUS WOMAN

You teach people how to treat you. It may be working for your Kgomotso to be jealous because you are paying her off. They get a control fix every time you reassure them, every time you answer the phone to report on your whereabouts. If she calls you 10 times to check on you, answer the phone once to offer information, then turn it off. Stop reinforcing their behaviour. Although you don't want to pay your Lerato off for insecure or controlling behaviour, you should be an open book. People with nothing to hide, hide nothing. Respect your partner enough to let her know where you are, when you will be back, and what you're doing.

DON'T LET FEAR RUIN YOU

I have learnt from my past relationships that women let their fears stop them from leaving what they have and finding love. I turned to understand that most women fear to be alone so they'd rather settle for this person who "kinda" loves them but really doesn't love them the way they love him! Don't get me wrong, women don't want to be alone because they are not happy with themselves and don't love themselves enough to be alone till they find love. They think maybe this corrupted love they have is the best they can do or maybe this is what they deserve, so they stay and let their feelings of fear rob them of happiness.

(FEAR OF THE UNKNOWN . AS HUMANBEINGS WE GO THROUGH THE WHAT'S IF QUESTIONS. WHAT IF I LEAVE WILL I FIND SOMEONE ELSE; WHAT IF I LEAVE AND FIND A MUCH WORSE PERSON THAN HIM. THE WHAT IF QUESTION HOLDS US BACK. AKA FEAR OF THE UNKNOWN.

A strong woman is a person who can leave a toxic relationship and find love, because it's tough to leave a person you love even when they don't love you the way you wanted them to love you. A weak woman is a person who lets a toxic relationship kills her ability to love and be loved and believe in love. Choose love over fear! Don't let your fear controls you...

COMMUNICATION 101: LADIES

In my past relationships, the most difficult and possible cause of break ups have been lack of communication. I have discovered a stark contrast between what each sex thinks the opposite sex wants from them, and what the opposite sex really does want. What women think men want from them causes women to have resentment and anger toward men, and feel hopeless about ever developing a wonderful, warm, romantic partnership. What men think women want from them causes them much of the same feelings and frustration.

The sad part is that it needs not to be this way, if only we would realize that both men and women are human beings first and pretty much want the same thing. But, you don't have to take my word for this. Honest communication is top priority for men. They want a woman who answers questions honestly, and perhaps even volunteers' information. You talk to Keabetswe, and she answer "whatever, I am fine or its okay. They want a woman who confidently asks for her wants and needs to be met. They want a woman who can see the truth and tell it like it is while communicating with kindness. Men want a woman who can communicate without being too critical, who cares about preserving his and her dignity. Women think men want them to be superficial, to keep quiet about their needs or wants, and never to ask for anything. Women think that men believe them to be too needy and too sensitive, and that men simply want women to get over it. Some women believe they do not have the permission to tell it like it is that they will be rejected for speaking up.

Great men want and need straightforward, courageous communication without anger or criticism. One way to attract a great man and build a satisfying relationship is to learn how to communicate your truth and needs effectively. Men want a woman to choose them out of need rather than out of desperation — either materially or emotionally. Men need to be wanted and needed by their partners, but they want their partners to have a separate identity. Men want a woman to be active and independent, to have her own friends and interests. Women think men don't want women to need them. Women think men do not need or appreciate time spent together as a couple. Women believe that showing a man he is needed will turn him off and possibly make him run away.

Men want what women want — a whole partner. One powerful way to attract a great man and build a vibrant relationship is to create a full, rewarding life for your own fulfillment. Men want no manipulation of any kind. They do not want to read their partner's mind or try to interpret signals. They do not want to be forced to move faster in a relationship than they are ready."Lindi and Jabu are getting married, when are you popping the question." They do not want to be manipulated into taking all the blame for things gone wrong. They do not want to be on the receiving end of game playing.

Women think men want little or no communication, and the only way to get needs met is through manipulation. Women think men either need or want to be reminded that the relationship needs to move forward. Women think men don't want or value praise and acknowledgment, and so tend to only verbalize criticism. Remember communications is a two way process, say what you would want said to you. And since you know what he wants, remember The desire to love and be loved is the most basic human need. Do you know how deeply God loves you? You are beautiful, loved, and not alone. Take a minute to think about that – God loves you, and not because of what you do. You don't need to act or look a certain way to be loved by God. He loves you unconditionally already. God created you and He is interested in the details of your life. God wants to have a close and personal relationship with you.

BAD ADVICE FROM THANDI

I usually hear women advise each other in taxis or nje by the fences or sending messages. Ladies, why? I would like to warn women to stop taking bad advice from other women who don't even have a good man in their own lives but are quick to give advice on what type of man to find!

A good man's job is not to pay for your car, bills and tab in the club, a good man is not looking to adopt a child, he's looking for a partner and a team mate. Men who rarely mind paying all these things for you are usually those who think they have a right to sleep with you because he's been handing out cash and doesn't even intend on being committed to you because they gave you all the money. A good man will not expect all the crap you come with, do you know why? Because he doesn't expect you to accept all his crap, so he gets his house in order for you and he expects you to do the same, otherwise u will lose that good man, he won't stay! A man who can claim you in front of your family, walk hand in hand in public, sleep next to you everyday and take you to exotic vacations is a man who can still cheat on you. So all these things don't make a man good... a good man is a faithful man first before anything! KNOW THE DIFFERENCE. And lastly, I find women concentrating too much on sex than they should. How do you make a good man from a man with a bigger front? We are so busy chasing good sex without even understanding that if you find a man with a bigger zipper but he's not faithful that means you are at a higher risk of STDs and babies outside your relationship.

STOP LISTENING TO BAD ADVICE THAT SOUNDS GOOD BUT HAS NOTHING TO DO WITH LOVE AND WON'T EVEN GET YOU A GOOD MAN!!

FOLLOW LOVE

I always hear people and songs that say "I feel it in my heart that he is the one." No I refuse, do not follow your heart, but follow love. Don't trust your heart. Control it! Why? Because your heart will let you fall in love with a married person. Your heart will make you cheat on your partner. Your heart will let you fall in love with a heart breaker and your heart can make you fall for two people at the same time! So why follow your heart? Doesn't your heart put you in situations where it hurts itself? So why trust it?

Protect your heart because it is not as wise as you are. DON'T FOLLOW YOUR HEART BUT TELL IT WHERE TO GO! You can't choose who you have feelings for but you can choose who to spend your life with. You can choose which relationship you allow your heart to enter. Control your heart and allow your heart to only enter a relationship with a person who understands Love is about being kind, gentle, faithful and honest! Give your heart to someone who loves you back! We tend to love people who we have feelings for because we followed our hearts and if that person doesn't love you back, you get hurt and then we blame love not our heart for taking us to the wrong place! You must tell your heart to wait and only go where love is because that's where your heart will never get hurt. Don't trust your heart trust in love! Don't follow your heart...

FOLLOW LOVE! IT WILL KEEP YOUR HEART HAPPY

I HAD MY FAIR SHARE OF GETTING HURT AND HURTING

This may come as a surprise to most, but what you're about to read may not be what you've known guys to be. I've been in a fair amount of long-term relationships where I've been "in love," or what I thought was being "in love," and then getting my heart broken. So here it goes...

I've learned to carry myself strongly through my past heartache. But wait... "A guy getting his heart broken? That doesn't make sense." Right? No. Wrong. See, guys are afraid to admit they've had their heart broken. They don't want females to see their vulnerable sideof them, which in turn pushes most girls away. But indeed, a lot of guys have had their heart broken.

Universally, the hardest part about heartbreak is

staying strong through it all. There aren't many people who can just get dumped and just say, "Ahh, screw it," and mean that honestly. When you get your heartbroken, it's hard to live with. It's hard to cope with. Someone who you once loved, and possibly still love, has broken and damaged you. You feel vulnerable. You feel like the only person in the world is that person who broke your heart.

But really, are they the only person for you? Probably not. See, if someone is able to break your heart, then that just shows that they're not the one you're meant to be with. Just before I got married, I was dating this girl for about a year and a half, and I was head over heels in love with her. I thought everything was great, except for the fact that I didn't get along with her parents, but we'll leave that out of the picture. I'd include all of that into this, but they and I just didn't see eye to eye because we came from two different worlds. Anyways, my girlfriend when Fifi was like my best friend...my ONLY friend, but we fought day in and day out. All day. EVERY DAY. It was wearing on both of us, but we knew we wanted to be together or so I thought. She went behind my back seeing this other guy before breaking up with me. Long story short, I had my heart broken because my ex wasn't happy and needed someone to jump to after her and I broke up.

I was torn apart. There was nothing on my mind more than fixing the relationship I once had with her, but I eventually learned that her and I just weren't meant to be together, even though she came running back to me a month later. Walking with your head high after a break up is hard to do. But every relationship is trial and error towards discovering who you're going to spend the rest of your life with. Some of us seem to forget that. Every relationship I've been in, I've learned something about myself. I've learned more about relationships. I've learned to build a wall, but not a full wall. Half a wall. Like a 6 foot wall. Something that someone can climb over and get inside of this fort I trapped myself in. Something that was doable, but it would take some hard work, effort, and dedication. This "mini fort." See, some people get their heart broken so many times that they think love is impossible to truly discover. FALSE. You just didn't find the right love yet. Don't let your guard down with every person you get with.

Keep your heart strong, and your brain smarter. Don't let yourself get heartbroken. That's easier said than done, but it's doable.

As a guy, I've had my heart completely shattered a few times, and it's the worst feeling ever. But I've faced that adversity, and I've bettered myself through each trial and tribulation. There's nothing better than taking every experience in life and turning it into a positive outlook no matter how bad the relationship may have been. There's always something positive to gain out of a negative experience.

Learning is a key part of life. And learning how to handle yourself is the best thing you can do for yourself. Eventually, you'll find someone that can handle themselves individually, but until that time comes, walk with your head high and your heart strong because there's someone out there for everyone. Find that person who allows you to be yourself and has no problem with anything you do. Find someone who doesn't want to change you. Find someone who makes you want to change yourself. To better yourself. Don't let negative previous relationships ruin your next relationship.

Love comes in the most unexpected situations and the right love, well... You'll just know when it comes to you. Guys (and girls), walk with your head high and your heart strong. Love yourself and others will love you. Bad experiences result in the greatest of learning lessons. Take it and run with it. Carry yourself stronger than you ever have. Let people love you for you, and not for who they want you to be.

Everyone has a past. Everyone is imperfect enough to mess up sometimes; never be ashamed of the scars that remains - give people the truth. Those who truly loves you will embrace you and mark the growth that comes with every lesson you learn. Never forget to give love without measure and apologize for hurting those you love.

CELLPHONES AND RELATIONSHIPS

Even with the most devoted couples, it seems that once-common conversations in bed have been replaced with endless scrolling through social media apps or funny image-based sites — individually.

Is the internet putting up a barrier between people, even in bed? We compulsively carry our smartphones with us wherever we go. The classroom, the bathroom, the bedroom, the outdoors — our phone is always in hand as if it were some magic self-defense tool capable of protecting us from all that is evil in the world. It all happened so fast. We didn't have the time to set any boundaries for smartphone usage, and now we find ourselves unable to save our relationships and form meaningful interactions with those dear to us. Smartphones are very useful in many circumstances. However, although not ruining your relationships per say, they can harm it in devious ways. To sustain a relationship it needs to be based on constant give and take, where we think about someone else at least as much as we think about ourselves. Smartphones upset this balance.

They can turn us into selfish, non-empathetic individuals who are only worried how many likes their Instagram photo received, or how often their meme got re-pinned. We place too much emphasis on our digital lives, and we lose sight of the urgency and beauty of the everyday.

If you don't want your partner to monitor your phone, messages, Facebook etc. you need to understand for your partner not to monitor your actions and whereabouts, is a privilege given to you because you are honest and loyal. If you are unfaithful then your partner generally takes that privilege away from you because you have broken the trust they had for you. Some people break the trust in the relationship then complain when their partners become super detectives. Trust is not a standard, it's a privilege

BEING FAITHFUL IS CONSIDERED STUPID

When you are faithful to you partner, others considers it as you being bewitched or you are a fool. Today I am considered a fool because I will not entertain other women. When women try to flirt with me and I don't entertain them, I am not rewarded for it. Women don't come up to me to tell me that it's good that I am faithful and I should keep it up. Instead I am accused of being gay because I don't give into another woman's seduction. They want a faithful man and then become amazed when I don't want to cheat on my woman, in fact it makes them want more of me and I think that's disrespectful. I am no longer considered cool because I am no longer a player and a bad boy. When other woman approaches me with no strings attached Vibes; I say no because I love and respect them more than they respect themselves. I say no because I perceive them as my sisters and I don't believe a woman should sleep with a man just for fun nor should a man sleep with a woman for fun. To my surprise I'm an idiot for turning down such an opportunity. I'm accused of not being man enough to handle "this"; we wonder why good men are rare to find?? It's just hard to be a good man with this entire disrespect going around and it's also hard to be a good faithful woman these days because most men take it for granted, which is also disrespectful. We just don't encourage and respect each other's relationships anymore.

Not all women but most women I come across today disrespect my relationship; it's like faithfulness is the new thing to destroy. Today my faithfulness to many woman is considered stupid and unpopular. To me, faithfulness is the foundation of love and no amount of hate and disrespect will change me from being faithful to one woman.

CHAPTER TEN

YOU BELONG

When you try too hard to belong or fit in with people, you'll end up hurt and rejected. Rather be rejected for who you authentically are, than accepted for who you pretend to be. Who you really are is the one thing that will never change but who you can become and what you may accumulate will change. In life, choose to be where you are appreciated and celebrated not where you are tolerated. Some people can live in your heart but not in your life, be okay with that reality. You are not money; not everyone will like or want you.

Remember to define your worth and value through the eyes of your Creator who calls you a delight and the apple of His eye - you are created to bring Him pleasure. Remember your strengths and magnify the value you add, by just being yourself and not seeking approval or validation from the next person. Surround yourself with people who believe in you, people who love you and npeople who value you instead of forcing yourself into the company of people who do not really appreciate your worth. Above all, remember that there is only one you and you need to look after that person, be kind to them and treat them with respect. That you are alive means that you belong; celebrate your worth.

DO YOU DESERVE HIM?

You can search throughout the entire universe for someone who is more deserving of your love and affection than you are yourself, and that person is not to be found anywhere. You yourself, as much as anybody in the entire universe deserve your love and affection." Buddha You can never keep something you don't deserve.

Most of us are looking for true love, but not all of

us will keep it once we find it. You see not all of us who are looking for love deserves to keep it. Why? Because some of us don't have love but we want love. We are looking for the right partner but we are not right ourselves.

Some of us are still caught up with our ex's but we are still looking for love somewhere else, others are busy flirting with other people yet we looking for someone who is not busy with others? Some of us abuse, cheat, lie, have bad tempers, swear when angry but we are looking for someone calm, gentle, honest, faithful and sweet. We spend time looking for love and some of us can't find it because we are looking for something we are not. It doesn't matter who hurt you, if u are still looking for love you must remain the person you are looking for. 50% of us looking for love, don't have love just excuses why we are hurt blah blah blah. We all have been hurt you are not special. What's special is a person who remains a good partner after being hurt, waiting for the right partner.

Love does not stay with anything less than love, so if u are looking for love and you don't have love yourself then love will see you are a fake and leave you eventually. You cannot keep love if you don't have love yourself, the truth will come out trust me!

You can never keep something you don't deserve.

CHAPTER TEN

TAKE IT FROM ME OR LEAVE

"A new command I give you: Love one another. As I have loved you, so you must love one another." Jesus Christ

TO YOU MY BROTHERS

My brother, I know that sometimes we take things and our friends for granted, but a friendly and brotherly warning, never ever take a woman for granted if she is giving you too much attention. Just consider yourself lucky because maybe, I mean maybe she loves you so much that she doesn't want anyone to take her place in your life. If she cries for you don't think she is weak but consider yourself lucky that she thinks you are worth her precious tears. If she is jealous of the other women around you don't think she is insecure but she doesn't want to see anyone else to be in your arms. My brother, if a woman says sorry to you even though it's not her fault, don't think she fears losing you, but she considers her relationship worth another chance and she wants no one else to have your heart. And if she is mad at you, hold her and kiss her and assure her that it's okay.

TAKE A LEAD

How does a man get a woman who will allow him to lead, and still remain by his side?

=ONLY THROUGH LOVE!

A woman can follow a man who leads with love. She trusts you to lead because she trusts your ability to lead with love. However, the problem is men think a woman must just follow regardless of how he treats her. "Because I'm the man" he says. But I ask you as a man, can you follow someone by your own free will if you don't trust them? If not, then how do you expect a woman to follow u while you keep hurting her? When you cheat on your woman, you have no idea do not understand how deep it cuts her. She begins to doubt doubts your leadership. She loses trust in your ability to lead her and doesn't trust that you or the decisions made by you, also consider her feelings and well being. A man who leads a relationship with love, will protect his woman from harm, he will not abuse her, be unfaithful to her or take her for granted.

But instead, he will treat her like the only precious diamond. From man to man I'm telling you that my woman allows me to lead because she can see I lead with love. And that's how you get a woman who is your partner to follow you by your side as your other half and equal. A king leads with his queen by his side, but a king treats his queen with love because he knows his nothing without her. A man is a leader. BUT ARE YOU A BAD LEADER? If you are bad one, you need to you must know that no woman wants to follow a bad leader from her own free will, because she don't trust you to have her best interest at heart. If you want a woman to follow you by your side, you must win her trust and the only way you win her trust is by vowing not to hurt her, especially intentionally, and continue to loving her for the rest of your life.

IF YOU LEAD WITH LOVE, SHE WILL FOLLOW WITH LOVE!

TO YOU MY BEAUTIFUL SISTERS

Why some women can't find love?

Answer: By not understanding what's providing.

Providing is making sure that the household or relationship is intact, making sure the bills are paid for and food to eat. Providing is not buying a woman weave and buying her flowers - that's pampering!! Providing and pampering are two different things. Women are leaving good men who can provide, for a man without morals who can pamper them. Because they told themselves that a man who doesn't pamper is not a man?? Did your mother give you that definition of a man or media?

It's funny how some women choose what they want as 50/50 and then what they want a man to do 100%, as Some women never pamper their man but want to be pampered because they have linked pampering to providing? Instead of seeing pampering as a mutual expression of love!! A Two way street!! Wake up!!

Pampering is a bonus not a standard!! Look for standards because there are a lot of men who have bonuses With bonuses but no standards!! A marriage without pampering will survive look at most our parents. But a relationship full of pampering without standards and morals never survives. As I said to To the men, this is not being selfish. If you are unable to cannot love yourself you are unable to cannot love someone else. Women often have trouble with this because they spend too much time loving others. They can airbrush themselves out of the picture and use up all their love on their man, their children and others. Loving yourself is the basis of life and the basis of a balanced personality. How can you take another's love for you seriously if you don't belief you are worth loving? If you can answer that question, them it's time to love your man, regardless of his social standing and looks. When he orders you to make tea or coffee, just do it, no questions ask. He wants to feel fresh to listen to your nonstop talks. Love him if he looks at all beautiful females, he is just checking that you still the best. Love him if he criticize your cooking, he is still improving his taste. Just love him if he snores at night and disturb your sleep, he is trying to prove that he is the most relaxed person since he met you and that actually also helps to chase the witches away. Love him if he forgets to give you a gift on your birthday or anniversary, he is saving for your future. Love him because you do not have a choice and remember killing is illegal. All you need to you must do my sister, is to love him and assure him and make him feel as the only man alive. Love him without restrictions, trust him without fear, want him without demand and accept him for who he is, and he will love you back unconditionally.

Just Love Him For Himself, Men have many qualities we love, perhaps they're strong, or sexy, or inspirational, or funny, or even rich. Understand that this is not why you love him, you love him just because of him, nothing else. Your love is not conditional, it is not based on any special qualities. You love him. Men, however, often think that it's their special blend of qualities that attracts you. Encourage your man to understand that it's not those qualities but their being themselves that you love. This is so crucial in knowing how to love a man.

Live In your Femininity whilst you may want to impress the man you love you must not stop being the woman you are. Your love should come from inside yourself, from your very soul. The love must be part of your femininity — however you express it — and be part of how you live. Remain just who you are, be the woman he met and fell in love with, that's how to love a man. He finds excitement in your femininity, particularly when it laced with love. Don't ever let him down. Remember, as a woman, just like Esther, Mary and Sarah, Never give up on anything that God has promised you. God seldom does majestic things in a hurry; exercise patience. He will do what He said He will do. God is honest; He has integrity and does not change His mind. Do not get discouraged when the deadlines you have set for yourself pass, do not worry when you see things that you never planned or budgeted for happen, don't fret. God restores, He heals and He delivers. Don't spend time thinking of the reasons why things happen they way do, the only thing you can do about something that has already happened is to accept it and deal with it. Learn from it and choose to grow from the experience. Your plan differs from God's plan so surrender to His will and His way of doing things and you will hold your peace. Know that just because something is God's plan does not mean the journey will be easy, but His grace is sufficient enough because where you are weak, God is strong.

Think of the fruit we eat. It starts its journey as a seed being buried underground, it draws nutrients from the dirt it is covered in until it sees the sunshine. The rains grow it, the winds don't uproot its tree. The same God who protects and provides for that seed, cares about and is devoted to you. Fear not, God will protect and perfect that which concerns you. Don't look around, keep your focus above. Look confidently to Him who knows neither failure nor defeat. Rest in the promise and you will live. Remember both species have different ingredients for successful relationships. A good man offers the same values his looking for in a woman. A bad man just wants a good woman with no values to offer. Notice the selfish mentality. A good woman offers the same values she is looking for in a man. A bad woman just wants a good man with nothing to offer him. Notice the selfish mentality. A successful relationship is when a good man and good woman offer values they have. They are both faithful, loyal, kind, gentle and are willing to work will work hard at building the relationship. A doomed relationship is when a good man is with a bad woman or a bad man is with a good woman. WATER AND OIL DON'T MIX! Find love and grow the love!!

LOOKS ARE A BONUS, NOT A NECESSITY!!

If you could see how women react when they see the so-called "hot guy"…mmmhhhh. You liked Tumelo because he was the hottest. His looks got your attention. But what made you fall for him was the fact that even though every girl wanted him, he choose to give you the attention. You gave him the opportunity to love allowed him to love you and eventually, you loved him back. But his biggest mistake was thinking he could mistreat you and get away with it. He allowed other girls to disrespect you. His side dishes kept blasting your phone, telling you how you are disrespecting their relationship with him. He never stood up for you. In fact, he He didn't see any reason saw no reason to apologise. Knowing that he hurt you, he still goes on to entertain entertains the side dishes, while his leading you on and standing you up, every opportunity you give him to explain himself, and eventually, decides to call calls you and tell he proposed to his side dish.

But then, you get the other guy. Ordinary. Not thaaaaaat good looking but definitely lookable. Respectful, kind, loyal, funny, caring, ready to 'kill' any man who tries to take a 10th look at you (by the way, not the obsessive kind of man), a man who just wants to love the you NOW and not the you that you will be. The kind of man to kiss your forehead and make the whole world know that you are his. The man who will call to order ANY person who disrespect you. He doesn't make you uncomfortable by looking at other females, and his aim is to simply make you happy.

IS ATTRACTION NECESSARY IN A RELATIONSHIP?

TO WOMEN: No man is going to understand will understand you when you get too comfortable in the relationship. If you take time to look pretty, paint your nails, keep in shape, kiss him when he least expects it and likes it, then you need to you must keep doing those things at least once in a whilesometimes. Why? Because you did those things to get him in the first place. You the one who introduced him to those things and if you stop, it looks like you were pretending. Don't be lazy and expect a man to stay because you say he loves you...attraction is still needed in the relationship and without it you put him in an uncomfortable position in your relationship. DON'T DO THAT!

TO MEN: your woman loves going out with you and being indoors with you too. She loves your attention; she loves those small things, like sending an SMS telling her how you feel about her, she likes that you keep in shape and are well groomed.

Whatever you did in the beginning initially to make her fall for you, you must keep doing it if you want a lasting relationship. Don't think her saying she loves you will make her understand why you taking away the things that made her love you in the first place. Attraction is still needed in the relationship and without it you put her in an uncomfortable position in your relationship. DON'T DO THAT!

Love is being the best version for each other! it's not being lazy and just saying we love each other, it's about putting the work to still be attractive to each other in the relationship. You both will define what is attractive in your own relationship as a couple and then commit to being that for each other. Don't stop loving each other!! Be the best for each other!

LOVE HAS NO SIDE DISH

We have become slaves to our emotions, our feelings rule us and that's why we compromise and settle for less than we deserve. We enter complicated relationships by falling for people who are in relationships and marriages. We justify our actions by calling it love but we know deep down inside we are being controlled by our feelings. Our values and morals are compromised because we allow our feelings to rule over us. Since when was a woman's love helping another man break his commitment to his woman? Since when was a man's love sleeping with other woman? Since when? Since when was love sleeping with other people when you both promised to be committed?

Don't you see that your feelings have driven you to be a liar and a selfish person? Why do you allow your feelings to be the master of you? As long as we keep allowing our feelings to rule us, we will keep hurting other people and calling it love. We will keep lying and being selfish all in the name of love, when love has always been identified by doing right by others. We were not created to be ruled by our feelings. Our purpose in life is to rule over our feelings. If we can master that we will not settle for nothing less than love and we will love back what loves us.

Love has no side dish.

FIND YOURSELF FIRST

It's easy to love and it's easy to say to a person I love you or its over. But the question I usually ask my friends is, how do you heal a broken heart? Do you know what Thabo wants after the love is gone? Do you know what makes Nomvula to be in the situation you in, and how to fix it? And well in many instances often I will not find the correct answer, or is there a correct answer?

It's easy to delete a number, ignore a call or cry for help, deactivate an account and or to unfriend someone on Facebook or in real life but moving on and erasing that person from your heart often seems impossible. Don't lose yourself trying to fight or get away from your truest self. Love, when it is genuine, is rarely easy because people have loved and been hurt, people have loved and been rejected and people have loved and disappointed. So by and large, love has been synonymous with pain, rejection and disappointment. The only way to heal a broken heart is to love. Anything that is broken is open.

Open to heal, open to receive, open to love. Love truly grows when you hold it closer when it hurts the most. Even God is near to the brokenhearted, He binds up their wounds. When I do my Sunday show on radio, I always say, "God is love." In expressing and preserving true love, you must decide to constantly bind that which is broken and remove that which breeds insecurity because perfect love casts out all fear.

A fulfilling love relationship where two people grow together as one, is not about having a hunky boyfriend or a hot girlfriend, though both can be awesome. It is not about trying to make things perfect because there are no perfect relationships but there is a perfect love. That love is perfect for the two who are in it but others rarely understand it: it is unique, it is rare and it is created and built specifically for the two people in it to enjoy. Nothing and no one is perfect so a perfect relationship does not exist. Perfect relationships only exist in Isibaya, Generations or Muvhango. Those love stories were written by scriptwriters but yours is written by God. The perfect love is born and successfully grows when two imperfect people make the daily commitment to, as best they can, love each other perfectly. This love is about finding and being with someone who compliments you, one who is strong where you are weak and then choosing to consistently and continually accept the worst in them, going through everything without giving up on them. Even God's strength is made perfect in our weakness. Love is patient and kind, it is long-suffering and keeps no record of wrong. Love forgives all things, bears all things. Be the perfect lover and you will attract the perfect love, but remember that love hurts sometimes when you do it right. Don't be afraid of a little pain, pleasure is on the other side. Be sensitive to your beloved's emotions, do not harden your heart to their cry no matter how insignificant it may feel or seem to you. There's always some truth behind 'just kidding', an element of knowledge behind 'I don't know', real emotion behind 'I don't care' and deep pain behind: 'It's okay". Never deafen your ear to subtle communication of discomfort or dis-ease in love, pain unattended breeds brokeness, chaos and discord. Love is made great but attending to the little, seemingly insignificant things. Love and life spring from and are driven by the heart. Look after your partner's heart. A person can be brain-dead and live, but all life ceases when a heart stops beating. By God, we were given: Two hands to hold, two legs to walk, two eyes to see and two ears to listen but only one heart. Each person was only given one heart because the other was given to someone else for us to find. Locate and follow your heart in another person because in so doing, you will have truly found yourself. After finding your other self, choose to live, to love and to grow together but as one. Be the love of your life, you are your own lifetime companion. Going after a dream has a price. It may mean abandoning your usual routines, it may make you go through hardships, or it may lead you to disappointment. But however costly it may be, it is never as high as the price paid by people who don't live. Have the courage to live and dare to love but always remember that your greatest, most loyal love lives, in you.

I am no expert in relationships, but there are simple rules to good relationships: Talk about things, the good, the bad and the Ugly. Be honest, faithful and be there for one another. Leave the past to the past, which includes ex's and old sagas. Just know that having an argument is part of growing up and it's normal. Ungakhohlwa. ..You won't be always happy. Don't expect change, be the change. We all have flaws, appreciate them. Appreciate umuntu wakho naye will do the same. Be best choomies and love each other unconditionally.

CHAPTER ELEVEN

CUT YOUR LOSSES

"A man never knows how to say goodbye; a woman never knows when to say it". Helen Rowland

I Always ask why women like keeping in touch with their exes, and the answer will be, oh no "Mongezi was a good guy", or "Thabiso is sweet", so why did you or did he dump you in the first place? It's a good question, and to answer, ultimately, I think its a bad ideait's a bad idea. First, your current partner isn't really going to like it, even if its well over between you two it's still THERE (eg you once f**ked them and worse, loved them) and in a way it's disrespectful to your current partner to still keep in regular touch. That don't mean if they have a baby with their new partner you can't say congrats, but emailing weekly or texting regularly is out of order. How would you like it? I don't understand why women keep in regular touch with ex lovers anyway. i know the whole thing about how 'we're still great friends blah blah blah' but surely people can hang out with other 'great friends' they haven't previously been intimate with? I believe in cutting my losses. We broke up for a reason, and why hang on, because that's really what it is, hanging on, not moving on. too many are people in denial. Holding on to previous romantic attachments creates feelings of distrust and can stymie an otherwise promising relationship. For instance, If you Stalk your ex on social media you not over them!! If u keep tabs on what they up to and who they dating or are they still single, you not over them!

    I for one don't even know if my ex'es are alive, why? Because they are not part of my life anymore, do u know if the man or women who lives 5km away from u is still alive? No...why? Because they are not part of your life, now do you wish people who are not part of your life dead? No! you wish them the best in life but u won't even know if they will receive that because u don't go around checking up on them, You'll only know if u bump into them by mistake. But my point is when you call someone your ex, just move on and stop watching them from the shadows! Like the songs says, "breaking up is hard to do," but that doesn't mean it isn't often necessary. There's no sense in wasting one minute of your time (or what's left of it) on an undeserving guy. Whether the break-up is your call, his call or mutual, cut your losses and start enjoying your life! You may be ranting and raving about how utterly selfish, cold and/or calculating Mbuso was when he wanted out of your relationship and there may be a lot of truth to your side of the story. When people feel trapped, they will often make very selfish and self-centered decisions by placing their needs before the needs of anyone else. Get over your ex!! Take that as a hint that you need to put your own needs first by leaving your EX alone. Rejection is never easy and begging for a second chance is hateful and disgraceful to your own soul.

If you Stalk your ex on any platform, be it social media you not over them!! If you keep tabs on what they up to and who they dating or are they still single, you not over them! I for one don't even know if my ex'es are alive, why? Because they are not part of my life anymore, do you know if the man or women who live 5km away from you is still alive? No, Why? Because they are not part of your life, now do you wish people who are not part of your life dead? No! You wish them the best in life but you won't even know if they will receive that because you don't go around checking up on them, You'll only know if you bump into them by mistake. But my point is when you call someone your ex, just move on and stop watching them from the shadows. Go on and find Find love. Sometimes you just have to you just must erase the messages, delete the numbers, and move on. You don't have to forget who that person was to you: You just have accept that they aren't that person anymore, Let GO! UZOMTHOLA OWAKHO.

On the 23rd of April 2016 I posted this on my Facebook page. Good Idea or Bad Idea: Remaining Friends with your Ex's Family?

Breaking up is hard to do, we all know it is, but if you spend any significant amount of time with your partner, chances are you you probably have grown attached to his family as well. But what happens if you want to remain close with your ex boyfriend's mom, or sister, or cousin? How would you feel if your ex kept his running lunch date with your dad? Although everyone's breakup and relationship is different, what I want to know is, do you think it is a good idea or a bad idea to carry on a relationship with an ex lover's family members?

Please give me permission to use your comments and quote you.

This were the answers:

"For me Is not a bad idea because you're not close to your ex its the family it will also depends on how far is that family the closer they stay the closer you will remain take it you're your relatives the ones near you are the closest not that you don't like others distance it will be the one to tell." Dr Oumakie Hlalele *"All has been said to add on that move forward with you new life I for one who is on that situation. Its painful I am married but my in laws are very closed to ex even if we have functions they are invited of which its so unfair for me. I wouldn't encourage that to happen to someone as I know the feeling."* Buyie Macele Ndlovu *"This is what is happening in my life. My first boyfriend still calling after 26 of the affair with their son from high school. They want me to attend any event with them. I got married and they gave me their blessing to a new man. I got divorced there are there for support. Their son even introduced me to his wife as one he should have married my parents denied.When there is something in the family his wife want to be next to me,I saw it putting the guy in a dilema when he wants to talk to her.But i am afraid to disappoint them when they invite me.And they always mention that he knows i am coming."* Maine Khomotso Khomo *"Don't tag my family, I won't tag yours let's move on!!!"* Puleng Mbhele *"Not a good*

idea. However having children leaves you no choice especially if your ex's family still like you. What done out talk about with your ex's family." Sibusiso Genge *"Okay, I think it is okay to be civil to them that all,I will use myself as an example my in laws all they could talk about it was thier son this and that . They just don't want to let go, for me I felt like I was in a cage they don't want me move on. So as for me 👎bad idea."* Manko Letsele *"Wooooow this is interesting.. What you asking is so happening to me as we chat…. my relationship with the mother , father . Sisters of my ex is unshaken I promise…. Just that i can't say much here."* Riri Omhle Duze *"Depending on the relationship both ex partners have with the Lord, I see no reason why that should be a problem. However, this will only work if the breakup was amicable. On the other hand, if If it was not, then my advice would be just to stay away from that family, unless both the individual and the family decide on a place to meet when they want to spend time together. After all, the The breakup was between the two parties concerned and not with the family. Hope this helps."* Julia Westmacott

"I'm still friends wth my ex's family and although I don't want to reconcile with him they have been like family to me and I still love them." Eleanor Summerton *"Eish I'm facing that the moment where I'm trying to cut the relationship with the family coz even when there is events I'm still invited how do to tell your current partner where u going well on my side its wrong to keep a relationship with them but harsh also harsh to give a*

cold shoulder its not easy." Desiree Lee Lawrence

"I will share my experience. I'm still in touch with them especially mamkhulu, we're still communicating. I cannot shut them like that, I'm not having a relationship with their son but them they still want to know I'm doing. But u must also communicate with your partner on how she feels about it." Jabu Manana-Zulu

"You used to wear size 5, now you wear size 8... Why do you want to hurt your feet by going back to that small size? Enjoy your current size. If everything is fine, that might be your size for life. Make home where you are." Sello Motloung *"It depends on how did the relationship ended. If there were no fights and name callings I see no issue why I can't be friends with his family. One will have to think of the current partners if they're open to this. It becomes difficult to the black society especially if ex is married and they have a traditional ceremony and boom here comes Pepetjie looking all fresh and sexy and Mrs current is sweating doing all the makoti duties."* Pamela Pepetjie Mthethwa *"Very interesting good question Mr Mbele how about the current Partner o new family."* Eliza Lizzy Mokoena

"Its a gud one, bt to be careful nr to hurt th current family, if u broke up wh r ex its him or her nt th family." Anna Moseme *"Keeping close to his family gave me hope that little hope that things might work out again i know its crazy right i mean he is married with his own family but keeping close his family its like*

having live souvenirs that just oh gosh where do I start I'm practically part of the family i will never get to own but never say never! Girl get grip on yourself he's about to walk with his family you need to you must be okay.... Me writing a scribble Bhuti Sipho I'm trying to portray here that other women really have a tough time letting go the Ex's family😭😭😭." Nalisu chocky Msane

"Let God guide you, and always remember what the scripture says. If U had a good relationship with them, why terminate it? U did not fight with them, but if Ur relationship with them was rocky even b4 ur divorce, it highly unlikely that it will improve. The only thing U can do is minimize the visits and the communication but when U meet them, be happy. Remember that there are children involved who will want to visit their Aunt, grandparents etc, and there will be special occasions where they will want to host a party for Ur kids, what then?, will u not support Ur kids just because the party is at their Grandmas house? Cutting ties will also harm the children because U will be forcing them to take sides and that is not what we want to teach our children. All U have to do is to ensure that the in-laws dont overstep their boundaries. Make rules to protect Ur feelings and emotions and also that of Ur

new woman. Making boudaries will ensure that there is less negative talk. If Ur in-laws are those that have bad family dynamicswith bad family dynamics, U may cut ties if they influence Ur kids negatively about U and Ur family, be civil and greet them when u meet. Good Luck with Ur book." Mmabatho Fakude *You can't just cut ties over night. Slowly over time it will happen naturally. relations between you and them should be kept civil especially if there are children involved."* Kelebogile Lebo Seopela *"My take remain civil with the ex's family, do not overstay move on, the illussion that you are the one may just be why you are holding o to this. Remember to give the other woman in his life a chance I am sure nawe you would not want an ex as your family in law."* Nomzamo Asakhe ladingwa-Mcoso *"If he still close to my fmly .really he still love me. and is depend how we broke up."* Mafahla Rikotso *"That's a very bad idea.....even if there's no bad blood between you and your exes family one should never be friends with his/her exes family,just to put your current partner and your exes partner at ease..you don't have to be enemies with them,you can still talk to them but don't be friends..they can be people that you know that you once had a close relationship with but it ended."* Nokthula Mthombeni

"I for one I don't think it's a bad idea what one must always do need to consider the current partner how will she/he feels with such matter. .Other than that I see no problem being friends with your exes family. .as long as u stay true n faithful to yourself." Gugu Mnyamane Mathebula *"Personally, I think it depends if the children already know this family....in this case it*

is okay to have a simple/decent relationship with your Ex's family." Tsiki Keswa *"I for one most the previous exs relatives they want nothing but to poke the present person or always call even if a fly passes they call you so that they make the present one jealous if many people get civilized and behave without offending the recent partner its fine but many are like mosquitoes that always zzzżzzzzz in the ear and they time wen the recent partner is around so if the relationship is dead so be it with the rest of the family."* Tsebe Mmanya *"Don't burn the bridges when we establish relationship we hope for the best not look at or anticipate the worst but oh well life happens & it's like a friendship cycle where you have strong bonds with one family than the other if they still perceive you like their own I don't see why not & let your partner know have an open dialogue & pray for God's guidance."* Laurentia L Sehume *"If the relationship is terminated I would not want to keep track on what my ex is doing, either success or downfall.....and keeping opening relations with the family will allow just that and them keeping track of what I'm doing."* Mamotetekoane Sebalabala

"According to me its a bad idea cuz the reason he knew them was through what we had and now that we are done let's move on." Blossoming Blossom

"If they are good people & there is no beef, yes otherwise NO!" Thandazile Mkhungo

"Personally i dont think it's a good idea. It would give some of

the other members a chance to pry into my present life. This is a case of letting bygones be bygones." Keneiloe Mogoli

WE DECIDE AND IT'S FINAL

When we find ourselves in situations as men, we usually do not call rarely call our gang or amajitha to discuss our sorrows, and 90 percent of the times, we don't even go to shrinks and we are even scared to approach our Pastors for help, unlike women. We usually deal with the pain is silos, maybe cry and sometimes end up taking take the wrong decision, yet walking away its always on our mind. These ladies , you have to you must believe, we then decide and when the decision is made, there is no turning back, you can call us dogs or whatever name but the decision has been made. And we do praypray. In all the decisions we make, we do invite invite the higher power. Most, if not all, the prayers we make, provoke God to give us opportunities. How you handle an opportunity determines if it will end up being be a blessing or a curse in your hands. Stop crucifying yourself for the past, or lamenting over what has already happened. We Don't fight too hard at or for anything. We Seek God and let His divine wisdom guide, protect and lead you. What you may see as an obvious way forward, God may see as a closed door. What you value as a priceless asset, God may want you to let go of. When you're looking for a clean break in life, a brand new start, a new beginning, refuse to let your past dictate to you. Make decisions Decide only on today because yesterday is gone, and tomorrow has not come. The confusion and fear and doubt you feel is because you're trying to do new things but seeing yourself as an old creation. Adjust your thinking to they way God sees you. Let Him be your benchmark and compass. You may feel stagnant yet the work He is doing inside you has taken you twenty giant leaps ahead of all your enemies and haters.

Make God your primary, most-trusted companion because He can never betray you or sell you out. In building something new you have to you must be with the right team. Leave everyone and stand alone with God so He can not only help, but also protect you. Wolves move in packs, but Eagles fly solo. Choose your happiness, your joy, your laughter above all else. Be true to yourself or you'll keep getting the short end of the stick. Leave and forget everything you know and believe only in the power that works in Christ and the promises in His resurrection. That same power lives in you. You decide to live your dreams, decide to be lead by God, and decide to be held by Him. Remain in the hold of your Creator. Proverbs 3v5-8: Trust in the Lord with all your heart, and lean not on your own understanding; In all your ways acknowledge Him, and He shall direct your paths. Do not be wise in your own eyes; Fear the Lord and depart from evil. It will be health to your flesh and strength to your bones.

HOW DO YOU KNOW HE IS THE ONE?

The mere fact that That you've been go out with Thapelo for the past year, doesn't mean he is the one and the love of your life. As I have said it before, find yourself first before you can even claim Thapelo to be the one, the love of your life. The love of your life is not the person you first loved or once deeply loved, it's the person who finally LOVES YOU BACK! They pour love into your life each day, which makes the uttering of the words "the love of my life" so easy. If they bring constant pain, turmoil and misery into your life, even when u love them, they become the "pain of your life". To move on and find love so you can call someone the love of your life is the only option. The dictionary says, "the love of your life is the person you want to spend the rest of your life with". But I'm saying to you, this will come natural when the person you love, loves you back. You can't spend the rest of your life with a person who only gives you pain, and more pain while you keep loving them. Look for a person who will love you back and love you more each day, so you may proudly say "the love of my life".

UMSHADO/ LENYALO

I have been asked this question many times, "Sipho, since you getting married again, how do you know that you are ready?" Ask yourself this: Is getting married right for you? What do you need to you must know before you say I do? I am not a relationship or marriage expert, but I think we can teach and learn from each other, from my past experiences. Why did you say "I DO" Be honest and evaluate the reasons behind your engagement. Write a list of pros and cons about your Tsepho and your relationship. If you have to you must talk yourself into marriage — don't. If you have to you must talk your fiancé into marriage — no way! Make sure you are Are not getting married to escape or avoid something. Have you just always wanted to get married? That's not a good enough reason. If you get nauseous shopping for a wedding dress or seem to be sick every time you have to you must meet the caterer, listen to your body. Don't be coerced like I was. I was even forced to learn French because of her business. Do you know and trust your Nosipho's personal history? The best predictor of future behavior is relevant past behavior. Learn from it. How Nosipho behaved in past relationships? How have they behaved with you? What has your partner learned about marriage from his/her parents? Look closely at your partner's parents — children learn what they live.

Have you planned a marriage — or just a wedding? Cake, flowers and fine dishes are all exciting, but there's more at stake than one day. Your wedding is a day; a marriage is a lifetime. You don't just want to be married, you want to be happily married. Think about the next 50 years. Put at least the same amount of time and effort that you are using to plan your wedding into planning your marriage. Develop an emotional prenuptial agreement with your partner, outlining how you'll handle children, discipline, sex, money, division of labour, religion, careers, retirement, in-laws, geography, etc. If you don't plan for and discuss these topics, you won't be able to successfully merge Merge two lives together. Take it from me I know. I was staying in Pretoria and she was staying in Morningside. She will come visit; yet we were married.

Are you investing more than you can afford to lose? Look at the cost of Look for your relationship. If you have to you must give up your friends, career, or family, for example, the cost is too high. If it all falls apart, are you going to be emotionally bankrupt?

It is better to be healthy alone, than sick with someone else. Have you identified and communicated your needs and expectations? Know yourself. You can't determine if somebody is good for you if you don't know your own needs. It's not selfish to have goals within a relationship. Express your needs and expectations now — not when you're already in the marriage. What are your absolute deal breakers? Don't rush, take your time.

"We must use time wisely and forever realize that the time is always ripe to do right." Nelson Mandela

CHAPTER TWELVE

PATIENCE IS VIRTUE

"To say that one waits a lifetime for his soulmate to come around is a paradox. People eventually get sick of waiting; take a chance on someone, and by the art of commitment become soulmates, which takes a lifetime to perfect."
— Criss Jami, Venus in Arms

Wait until you find love... I always wonder why people are afraid to be alone and jump into relationships after a failed one. I really do not understand why and who told them than we you are in love everything will be perfect. In my view, being Being a relationship is hard, it's like running a company. You think you can never love someone as much as you loved that person who broke your heart. But wait until you love a person who understands love. You will always feel like each day is a dream, each moment a fantasy because you can't simply understand how love can feel so good. To finally be with someone who loves you back and loves you each day not only by saying the words but also loving you by their actions. You think you can never love someone again and start telling yourself that love is just not for you. You think you will never love this deep. Wait until u find love! Love will take away all the hurt you've been carrying inside of you. Love will appreciate you, protect you, never take advantage but live to serve only for the greater good of your soul. You will have no choice but to love more and deeper than ever before because there is nothing as magical as a union of love. Wait until you find love!! Love is not a switch when people get hurt they say for now I just want to concentrate on my job or my studies then after that I Will start looking look for love again... Is love a switch that you can switch off and onafter graduation or a promotion at work? Can you control when love will find you? So why are you telling love when it should come? Are you a traffic officer of love?

Don't let your own pain ruin your life. You got hurt, but u not special we all got hurt but here we are still looking for love. I have never heard anyone have heard no one complain that love came to them at a wrong time because the truth is love can come at anytime and anytime is perfect to finally meet someone who loves you the way you love them.

So take the time to Heal and jump straight back into finding love. So you can see it when it comes and not let it pass you by because you are still studying or waiting for a promotion at work.

LOVE IS NOT A SWITCH!!

CHAPTER THIRTEEN

WHY STAY?

"A bad relationship is like standing on broken glass, if you stay you will keep hurting... If you walk away, you will hurt but eventually u will heal".

Autumn Kohler

Sometimes we have a completely irrational fear of being on our own, which in turn can keep us in a relationship well beyond its sell-by. But when you really stop to think about it, what's so horrible about spending some quality time with the one person we know we can at least agree with? In fact, some Some extended alone time can be really good for you. It's an opportunity to catch up on those things we've been not so secretly dying to do: maybe it's a night class, maybe some redecoration… it could simply be giving yourself the time to see those movies you missed. Best of all, though, it's a

Why Stay

chance to really get to know and understand yourself, and give you the chance to discover discover what it is you need and want from a relationship next time around. You stay because you don't understand love! If you don't understand love, you will keep going back to the person who hurt you and call it love, if you don't understand love you will let someone use you over and over again repeatedly and blame it on love, because you are calling ignorance, love.

A person who loves you, will never "keep" hurting and using you and saying I love you. U keep going back because you hold on to words and turn a blind eye to their actions! U keep hoping on to his/her words because you simply do not understand love. Love was never words. Love has always and will always be a verb.

LOVE IS AN ACT! So keep lying to yourself about what love is, but just know you will never be happy in life staying with someone who offers you continuous pain. Do not use love for your benefits, stay because you don't understand love!

NOTHING BUT THE TRUTH.

- There is nothing Nothing that threatens the security of a woman than the thought of another woman competing for the attention and affection of her man. Nothing is more painful. Nothing is more disrespecting. Nothing is more insulting. Nothing is more belittling and degrading.

- Relationship flourishes when the couple works together as a team; when both Thabo and Mmakoena decides that winning together is more important than keeping score. Good relationships don't just happen. They are a product of hard work.

- Your friends and families are watching you and forming lasting opinions on love, commitment, and marriage based on what they see in you. Give them hope. Make them look forward to love.

- MAN: The reason why other women look attractive is because someone is taking good care of them. Grass is always green where it is watered. Instead of drooling over the green grass on the other side of the fence, work on yours and water it regularly. Any man can admire a beautiful woman, but it takes a true gentleman to make a woman admirable and beautiful.

- When a Mandla puts Nothando first above everyone and everything except God, it gives her the sense of security and honor that every woman hungers for.

- A successful relationship doesn't require a big houserequires no big house, a prefect spouse, a million Rands or an expensive car. You can have all the above and still have a miserable relationship. It only requires honesty, undying commitment and selfless love and Jesus at the center of it all.

- Pray for your spouse every day; in the morning, in the afternoon and at evening. Don't wait until there is a problem. Don't wait until there is an affair. Don't wait until something bad happens. Don't wait until your spouse is tempted. Shield your spouse with prayer and cover your marriage with the fence of prayer.

- The people you surround yourself with have a lot of influence on your relationship. Friends can build or break your relationship; choose them wisely.

- One spouse cannot build a relationship alone when the other spouse is committed to destroying the other spouse will destroy it. Relationships works when both man and woman work together as a team to build it.

- Don't take your spouse for granted. Don't take advantage of your spouse's meekness and goodness. Don't mistake your spouse's loyalty for desperation. Don't misuse or abuse yours spouse's trust. You may end up regretting regret after losing someone that meant so much to you.

- Beware of advice from single people. Regardless of how sincere their advice may be, most of it is theoretical and not derived from real life experiences. If you really need Godly advice, seek it from God-fearing, impartial and prayerful mature couples whose resolve has been tested by time and shaped by trials.

- Dear Sister, Don't underestimate the power of the tongue on your relationship. The tongue has the power to crush your love or build it up. Don't let the Devil use your tongue to kill your spouse's image, self-confidence and aspirations. Let God use your tongue to build up your relationship and bless and praise your spouse.

CHAPTER FOURTEEN

GOD IS LOVE

Throughout life people will make you mad, disrespect you and treat you bad. Let God deal with the things they do, because hate in your heart will consume you too. Will Smith

So often in the face of trial and tribulation we forget that God is ever-present and ever-faithful, even though his word assures us that many are the afflictions of the righteous but the Lord delivers him from them all. We overlook God's presence with us and panic: we worry, we stress. We forget that we are created by Him who knows neither failure nor defeat. It skips our mind that He is the Lion of the tribe of Judah with victory in His blood. Good and evil work together to bring good, we should never fear when trouble descends, and we should never let trouble overwhelm us. Greater is He that is in you than He that is in the world; you will overcome. Prayer invokes God's presence, it releases His wisdom. God dwells in the praises of His people. Your faith in the Lord God Almighty is never in vain, it is the currency that you need to marry with endurance, patience and perseverance and you will emerge triumphant. Neither fear nor worry; God with you means you are always and automatically in the majority. Rest and Rejoice. Stop lamenting over all you may have lost, stop crying over all that's gone missing, stop feeling guilty over all that's been taken. In restoring you, in reviving you and in rebuilding you, God is only going to use will only use what you have still got not what you have lost. The only thing you can do about the past is accept it and learn from it. Regretting it won't change it and crying over it won't reverse it. Move up and move on.

Everyone makes mistakes in life, never let anyone let no one crucify you because they sin differently to you. Every saint has a past and every sinner has a future, stop hurting over things that are already done. Forgive others and forgive yourself, set yourself free. Do not continue in self-condemnation because nobody is perfect and thankfully nobody has to nobody must be, because God does not use any perfect personuses no perfect person, He qualifies the called, He fixes the broken and He heals the hurting. Trust God to see you through, especially in impossible situations, He will lead you, He will guide you and He will teach you. Stop doubting yourself, don't undermine your ability, do not look down on your intelligence. God can do what no man can do.

- Psalm 91v15, Hebrews 9v12: 15 He shall call upon Me, and I will answer him; I will be with him in trouble; I will deliver him and honor him. Not with the blood of goats and calves, but with His own blood He entered the Most Holy Place once for all, having obtained eternal redemption.

LOVE AND THE CHURCH

"I understood that the Church had a Heart, and that this Heart was burning with love." Therese of Lisieux Churches should preach more about love than about material things! This world will not get better if we all become rich. Our relationships and marriages will not become better because we receive bigger houses and nicer cars. So it's sad to see churches spend more time preaching about money, cars and houses. No amount of money will teach anyone to have respect and become more kind and gentle, only LOVE can do that! What is the greatest commandment? Is it not love? Then why do churches preach more and motivate more about materialism?

"What you spend most of your time on is considered to be more important"

God blessing you with a car and house is not bad and churches motivating people that God will bless them is not wrong. But we should know that materialistic things DO NOT bring us closer to God. Only LOVE brings us closer to God, even with a small house and cheap car; because GOD IS LOVE! So why spend so much time preaching about things that don't bring us closer to God? Big cars and houses don't solve our relationship and marriage problems only Love can, because LOVE SURMOUNTS EVERYTHING!

Let us preach more about love and counter attack abuse, disrespect, selfishness and unfaithfulness in our homes, because these are our biggest problems and our nation is perishing because of lacking the greatest knowledge, which is LOVE.

People must know and be aware that know that materialistic things don't bring happiness, only LOVE can do that.

GOD IS LOVE.

LET'S PRAY AND ASK GOD FOR LOVE

For the Lord has heard my weeping. The Lord has heard my plea; the Lord will answer my prayer. - Psalm 6:8-9 I pray for Mantwa's to find their Thabo's. For those who have lost love, who grieved, who healed, who bravely walked and moved forward, for those who have endured with their faith and gleaned the wisdom from the painful season, for those who have let with let go of their losses, faced their fears, and been honest with their mistakes, for those who have rejected the lies that they're not lovable, for those choosing to believe in love even though they have been disappointed or even been betrayed. I pray for you to find a love so true, so dear, so lavish, and so faithful...for love that is sweet and tender, but so safe and so holy. So divinely inspired and given from God. I pray you are celebrated, embraced, held and cherished...

That you are given the greatest blessing of having a life partner to share and grow and build and dream with -someone to love you in your weakest and strongest moments and everything in between. I pray your days of the past are redeemed; the sting of the pain being completely gone, just like a woman who has endured great pain and suffering in labor and given birth to her child that she has now instantly fallen so deeply in love with. Her pain is forgotten. I pray this happens for you and for me. I pray the men who have waited so long for their sweet Mantwa will no longer be lonely nor disappointed. That his arms never are empty. His life he's worked so hard to build will feel complete with her by his side. Have faith you will find love again. In my deepest, darkest moments, what really got me through was a prayer. Sometimes my prayer was 'Help me.' Sometimes a prayer was 'Thank you.' What I've discovered is that intimate connection and communication with my creator will always get me through because I know my support, my help, is just a prayer away.

CHAPTER FIFTEEN

FINITO

"Love is like a friendship caught on fire. In the beginning a flame, very pretty, often hot and fierce, but still only light and flickering. As love grows older, our hearts mature and our love becomes as coals, deep-burning and unquenchable."
Bruce Lee

If you are reading this part it means you are at the end like in the movies credits will come up or go down. I did a lot of good and bad stuff in my life, I cheated, lied, got drunk, been arrested, but love kept me sane. Whenever I would be in a relationship, I would truly love, I will be dedicated, yet cheat a little if I am permissible to say that. But truly if you can go back and ask all the girls I've loved before, they will tell you, I was loving and sweet. I think growing up changes a person, to either good or bad. Maybe I would have been dead now, but God is love kept me alive. As my neighbour, MaSkosana would say, "God really loves you my son."

Most of the challenges you are facing will go away when you just start to practice practice love and treat people well. Love your neighbour as yourself, treat people how you would like to be treated and remember that you reap what you sow. The greatest prayer you will ever make is how you treat people. You only get back what you put in. Quite often often we feel justified in bearing grudges, holding the wrong that people have done against us, we cling onto forgiveness because we have been hurt, disappointed or betrayed. Learn to forgive people and when you have done that, remember to set them free. No one is worth you not living God'sperfect plan for your life. Bless your enemies and pray for them, then you will have peace. You will take back your power and feel light. When a man's ways please the Lord, even his enemies will be at peace with him. Love is a free gift; give it.

They just promised it would be worth it I always say to my daughters, I know that I have been hard on you to do the best that still stands girls. And remember: Life is too short to wake up with regrets. Love the people who treat you right. Forget about the ones who don't. Believe everything happens for a reason. If you get a second chance, grab it with both hands. If it changes your life, let it. Nobody said life would be easy. I am father, a brother, a lover, a husband, all I need is love. So go out there and love the one you are with.

Love

Mbelesi.

ABOUT THE AUTHOR

Sipho Mbele, is a brother, friend, graduate from TNG (Now known as TUT), father and husband who is passionate about personal growth. He is the founder of Mbelesi Holdings, a company that manages artists and event coordination. A radio presenter with 20 years of experience, an actor who appeared in soapies and a couple series in South Africa. He is writing his own Movie, and busy shooting a drama series for television. Sipho is a motivational speaker, programme director and an event coordinator. He is fulfilled when he sees young people reaching their potential. His work includes Mc for Ms South Africa, featured on Muvhango, Jacobs Cross, Soul City 10, Mtunzini.com. Unexpected 2, Scandal and A slippery Life. He has been associated with renown Musicians in the Country, Brian Temba, Israel Mosehla, Afrika Mamas, Mighty Voices, Zodwa Mabena, Bathabile and Tshwane Gospel Choir just to mention a few.

A God fearing man and a motivational speaker. This is his first book, read and enjoy.

www.ingramcontent.com/pod-product-compliance
Lightning Source LLC
Chambersburg PA
CBHW031447040426
42444CB00007B/1009